SO-CGS-025

RAPE
What Would You Do If . . . ?

As a young woman, you must be concerned about and aware of rape. It could happen to you anywhere—in your own home, at a shopping center, on a date—and with anyone—even someone you know. The best ways to avoid being assaulted are to be knowledgable about rape and to be alert to potentially dangerous predicaments. Know how to make yourself safe at home and in other situations. Find out why men rape, and whether or not you should actively resist if you are attacked. Know what the medical, legal, and emotional aspects of rape are and where to go for help. *Every* female is a potential rape victim. Arm yourself with accurate information about rape and don't become another statistic.

BOOKS BY DIANNA DANIELS BOOHER

Coping . . . When Your Family Falls Apart

What Would You Do If...? RAPE

Dianna Daniels Booher

JULIAN MESSNER  NEW YORK

CORONA DEL SOL HIGH SCHOOL
MEDIA CENTER
1001 E. KNOX ROAD
TEMPE, AZ 85284

Copyright © *1981* by *Dianna Daniels Booher*

All rights reserved including the right of
reproduction in whole or in part in any form.
Published by Julian Messner, a Simon & Schuster
Division of Gulf & Western Corporation,
Simon & Schuster Building,
1230 Avenue of the Americas,
New York, New York 10020.

JULIAN MESSNER and colophon are trademarks of
Simon & Schuster, registered in the U.S. Patent
and Trademark Office.

Manufactured in the United States of America.

Design by Irving Perkins Associates

Fourth printing, 1983

Library of Congress Cataloging in Publication Data

Booher, Dianna Daniels.
    Rape : what would you do if—?

    Bibliography: p.
    Includes index.
    Summary: Explores the motives behind rape, potential
rapists and their characteristics, and the impact of this crime
on society. Also discusses ways of protecting oneself from
attack, and how to deal with an attack and its aftermath.
    1. Rape—Prevention.   2. Rape victims—Services for.
[1. Rape]   I. Title.
HV6558.B66   362.8'8   81-914
ISBN 0-671-42201-4   AACR2

*Thanks to my sister ANGIE
and my friends MELISSA and KIM
who helped with the manuscript*

Contents

PART ONE

Prevention— Be Alert

CHAPTER *1*

Attitude's the Thing

Amy, seventeen, hurried from the shopping center to her parked car. Both she and her friend had early dates that evening and were anxious to get home. Finding that the car wouldn't start, the girls decided to walk the few blocks home. Amy's friend, who had only thirty minutes to dress for her date, ran on ahead. Amy, who'd made a date for a little later, took her time. She watched nonchalantly as her friend disappeared around the corner ahead of her. A few minutes later, witnesses say, a car pulled up beside Amy and a man got out. He grabbed her arm and pulled her into the car. The following day, Amy's raped, nude body was found on a public beach. She had been suffocated with sand.

Kimberly, fourteen, home alone, heard the doorbell ring in the middle of the afternoon. She peered out a front window to see a well-dressed young man standing outside the door. Opening the door slightly, she asked what he wanted. The boy asked her if a Ted Simmers lived there. When she told him he had the wrong house, he lingered a moment and apologized. While they were talking, the telephone rang. He apologized again and walked back toward his car. Kimberly shut the door hurriedly and ran to answer the kitchen phone, it was a wrong number. When she walked back through the entryway, the boy who'd been at the door earlier stepped out from behind the corner, pulled a gun, and ordered her to walk with him through the rest of the house to look for anyone else who might be at home. Finding no one, he took her to the bedroom, ordered her to undress, and raped her. With her mouth taped shut and her hands tied together, she heard him drive away.

Sheryl, sixteen, trainer for her high-school girl's volleyball team and photographer for the school newspaper, arrived at the gym at about 9:00 Saturday for a volleyball tournament. She left her purse and equipment with friends while she went to the restroom. When the game started and she hadn't returned to the team's bench, her friends went to look for her. Her raped body was found behind some stage backdrops on the balcony of the school auditorium.

Donna, fifteen, left her house for school at 7:00 A.M. Her mother had asked her to walk her little brother to the nearby convenience store, where he wanted to buy baseball cards. She waited for him outside the store; when he came out, she sent him home. A few minutes later, while she was waiting at the bus stop, a boy she knew from school came by and asked if she wanted a ride. They talked a few minutes and then he repeated the ride offer. She accepted. But instead of driving her to school, the boy took Donna to a nearby park, where he parked under some shade trees near a locked, fenced-in area. Pulling her toward him, he began to kiss the back of her neck. She protested, telling him that she was dating someone else and that her boyfriend would be very angry. He told her to shut up, pulled a knife, and ordered her to undress. When he finished raping her, he drove her back to the bus stop. As she got out, he cautioned her not to tell anyone because he knew where she lived and he'd make her sorry.

These girls and most rape victims share one common attitude—they never think rape can happen to them. Yet statistics shatter that feeling of security. By some estimates, one-fifth to one-fourth of all girls will be sexually attacked sometime during their teen years. Sex crimes are the fastest-growing category of violent crime in our country. According to the FBI Uniform Crime Report, 67,131 rapes occurred in 1978, which means a rape took place in the United States once every eight minutes. In 1979, incidence of rape increased by 13.2 percent. The picture grows even bleaker when you realize that by FBI and private researchers' estimates, only one in ten rapes is ever reported.

The prime victims for these attacks are girls ten to nineteen years old. As a result of the research of Menachim Amir, who did the first major study of rape in 1971, and of later researchers, we can now throw away old myths about rape and look at the facts:

- Rape is primarily *intra*racial. Black men rape black women; white men rape white women.
- Rape occurs in all social classes, with rapists generally attacking victims from the same geographical area and economic class.
- The rapist is not always a stranger. In one-third of all

attacks, victims and rapists know each other. The estimate for "acquaintance" rapes goes even higher when you consider that most unreported rapes fall into this category.

- Being home and off the streets does not prevent rape. One-third of all rapes take place indoors, usually in the victim's home.

- Rape is not a result of unbridled sexual passion, committed on impulse. Both young children and the elderly are victims. Three-fourths of all rapes are planned ahead of time. The victim turns out to be whoever happens along at a certain place or answers the doorbell. Rape, meant to humiliate and degrade the victim, is an act of violence.

- Being with a group does not necessarily make for safety. Two out of five attacks are committed by a pair or group of males. Often parties are the scene of such attacks.

- Rapists are seldom "dirty old men." Rather, most rapists are fifteen to twenty-four years old. Offenders are usually five to ten years older than their victims.

- Rapists are not insane. When compared to other men in a similar category of the same race, age, economic and social class, psychologists can see no distinguishing mental disorders. Rapists do not stand out from ordinary men; they give victims no clues as to their intentions.

- "Nice" girls get raped. Years ago, the common idea was that all you had to do to avoid rape was to stay away from bad places and questionable friends, keep off the streets at night, and mind your own business. Girls and women who had been raped kept the incident a secret for fear of rejection by family and friends—as if the rape were a mark against their own moral character. Life-styles have changed. The average teen does not go straight home after school and stay there. She is involved in sports or club activities or works part-time. Being nice has little to do with avoiding rape.

With these facts of rape in front of you, perhaps you have taken the first step in rape prevention, which is to shed the attitude that rape can't happen to you. Rapes and attempted rapes happen to women of all races, classes, and ages.

Social conditioning may make it difficult for some girls to understand the viciousness of rape. Because we see reflections of our violent society in movies, magazines, and novels, we become numb to the reality. For others, the awakening of natural sexual drives during adolescence obscures the truth about rape. Most females begin at an early age to look forward to falling in love, and at some time during their early teens they begin to consider the beauty of sexual love within marriage. This is especially true when parents have provided a good model of the sexual happiness in marriage.

The difference, however, between this kind of sexual love and rape is too wide for description. Sex between loving partners in marriage is a pleasure; rape is pain, both physical and psychological. Physically, victims may suffer nausea, bruises, muscle soreness, cuts, damage to internal organs, unwanted pregnancy, venereal disease, later childbirth complications, and even death. Psychologically, a victim loses control of her emotional self. Her personal identity is violated. She suffers from fear—fear that she will be rejected by her family and friends, that she will have future complications, that her life will be in danger if the attacker returns. She often develops phobias surrounding some aspect of the attack—fear of the outdoors, fear of being alone, fear of men, fear of a ringing telephone.

The victim suffers from anger and rage at her helplessness to fight back or to control her own life. She often feels the need to change her entire life-style to avoid future attacks—to transfer to a new school, to move to a new city, to drop social activities, to change friends, to isolate herself from her parents in order to protect them.

Being naive about the fact that rape can happen to anyone and becoming desensitized to its effects make you more vulnerable. The right attitude about rape can ensure your future safety and the safety of others.

One thing you can do is decide beforehand that you will report a rape or an attempted rape. Often, after an attack, the victim is too confused to think clearly. Fear overwhelms her. She may just want to withdraw from the world for a while. Although this attitude is understandable, it weakens a victim's future well-being. Reporting a rape, by setting in motion steps to apprehend and convict the rapist, will help rid a victim of fear that the rapist will return, and may ensure that he is off the streets away from other potential victims. "Rape is a very repetitive crime," says Officer A. V. Montgomery of the Houston Police Department.

Since the women's movement has publicized rape and the how-to's of reporting attacks, the number of reported rapes has risen. A neglected area of emphasis, however, is reporting *attempted* rapes. That someone only *tried* to murder you and did not succeed should not lessen your rage. Rapists who unsuccessfully attempt rape should not get away to succeed the next time.

While doing research in the Denver area, Carolyn Hursch found that it did not even occur to many victims to report an attempted rape. Ms. Hursch advertised for victims of both rape and attempted rape to come forward to be interviewed. In studying the attempted rape cases, she hoped to find out how various victims talked their way out of an attack. Expecting more calls from victims of attempts than completed rapes, she was surprised to find just the opposite. Victims of attempted rapes hesitantly stated that they weren't sure the incidents were important enough to record. In other words, victims of attempts never fully realized what they had narrowly escaped. So decide now that you will report any sexual attack or attempted attack made on you.

The second thing you can do about rape is develop the attitude that you are primarily responsible for your own safety. Many people have suggested that society trains females to be victims. They learn to appreciate compliments and passes as if such remarks and actions from males proved their worth.

Girls are also taught that they are physically weak and incapable of taking care of themselves, that they need a brother, boyfriend, father, or husband for protection. But what about all the times a girl is alone? She must learn protection is her own responsibility.

Parents often warn daughters to watch out for the traffic or for poisonous toadstools, but they fail to warn them about potential rape situations and what to do about them. Perhaps they generalize with "be careful" because they're afraid to consider the real, specific dangers that their daughters face.

Whatever the reasons for naiveté, this book will help you to prevent rape. If you have already been attacked, the book can help you cope with rape's effects.

When I first discussed the contents of this manuscript

with colleagues, I was cautioned that warning girls about so many dangers may create paranoia. I took these comments to heart and began to revise my plans.

But as I interviewed more victims and checked information from police files, I became convinced that that's exactly what our society calls for—a good healthy case of paranoia about rape.

Change of attitude is the first step in rape prevention. Realize that you are a potential rape victim; take precautions seriously. If your attitude is right, you're ready for the specifics in the following chapters.

CHAPTER **2**

Safety Away from Home

Chances are that you've already been the target of an attempted rape and never knew it. As I talked to friends about this book and asked them to share their experiences of close calls, the first reaction was "I can't think of anything offhand."

Then as I mentioned some of the common lines of attackers, friends began to remember. Stories poured out of potentially dangerous situations, in which the potential victim never became aware of the danger because she had intuitively made the right response. Escaping, even through ignorance, certainly can't be knocked. But recognizing potentially dangerous situations is your best defense against attack.

Gail Pageant, of the Rape Crisis Center of Houston, says that vulnerability and naiveté are teens' chief enemies. Girls have not been made fully aware of potential dangers and, more specifically, of how to deal with them.

Of course, there's probably not a teen alive who hasn't been told, "Don't talk to strangers." You hear that from parents and teachers and see it in films about safety from kindergarten on up. The big catch is that no one ever tells you who the strangers are and what to do if they try to make you talk to them.

Anyone would be wary of a stranger who attempts to grab your arm, force you into a dark alley or building. A more subtle attacker often catches you off guard by trying to shed the "stranger" label. This rapist sets you up a few minutes or hours before the attack. He tries to win your trust and make you see him as just a nice guy being friendly. He works by "interviewing" his potential victim. If she passes the "test," he forgets her and looks for another victim. If she fails the test, he proceeds with plans for the attack a little later.

Dana failed the test. She worked as a clerk in a large department store two evenings a week and on Saturdays. One particular customer, Mr. Jackson, walked into Dana's department one evening while she was working alone. She asked if she could help him make a selection. Mumbling about looking for something for his daughter who was chubby and hard to fit, he flipped through the racks of girls' dresses. After a few minutes, he stopped looking and made a few pleasant remarks about how his daughter hated to shop and that he picked out most of her clothes. They chatted a few minutes about styles and finding a proper fit and about which stores had better selections. Then he left. "A nice, friendly man," Dana thought as he walked away.

A few evenings later, Mr. Jackson returned and greeted Dana by name. Her voice showed her surprise. "How did you know my name?"

"Your nametag." He gestured toward the white badge and grinned. Dana blushed and shrugged.

Mr. Jackson repeated the dress-rack routine, found nothing, and stayed to talk a few minutes. This and subsequent visits followed without Dana becoming suspicious. After all, Mr. Jackson had a wife and two kids, one of them a blind college-age son, Troy, who, his dad hoped, would someday meet a "nice young lady like Dana" to build his confidence.

A few days later, Dana was coming out of the library when a familiar voice called to her. "Hey, Dana, got a minute?

The voice came from a car parked near the library curb. She bent over and peered into the car to see Mr. Jackson.

"I'm waiting for Troy; this is where I pick him up. Have you got a minute to wait and meet him?" He shoved the car door open on her side.

"No, I . . . uh," Dana backed away, startled and ashamed of her fear, "I'm supposed to pick up my little sister from the babysitter's in a few minutes. I can't."

"Okay. Catch you next time, then." Mr. Jackson waved her on with a friendly, fatherly smile.

Dana scurried off, ashamed that she had been startled and frightened. At first, she thought she'd been followed and wondered how he knew where she was. Then she remembered that during their visits at the store, she had commented about coming by the library to study between school and work hours. He was just a nice man trying to matchmake for his blind son. She felt heartless and embarrassed.

A few afternoons later, Mr. Jackson appeared at the store and expressed regret that Dana hadn't had time to meet his son. Troy was so lonely and depressed, especially this semester because he was having trouble with his schoolwork. Mr. Jackson suggested that perhaps Dana could tutor Troy in math if his grades didn't improve.

One morning a week later, Dana sat in her car in the school parking lot studying for a first-period exam. She had closed her eyes to conjugate Spanish verbs when she heard the door open. She shrieked and looked up to see Mr. Jackson climbing in the car beside her. She stared and said nothing.

His smile was gone. In its place were tightly drawn lips, a steady gaze. He never spoke. He sat facing her, his breathing growing heavier.

"What are you doing here?" Dana asked.

He never answered, only stared.

"Dear God," Dana prayed to herself, "get this guy out of here. Now. He's crazy. Get him out." A carload of kids pulled in only a few spaces away from them. Dana reached for the door handle just as Mr. Jackson reached for her arm. She pulled away and got out of the car. Mr. Jackson jumped out the other side, returned to his own car, and drove away.

Shaken, and realizing at last that this wasn't a social call, Dana went to phone her dad, who called the police. As the day wore on, Dana was still unsure about the reporting. How could he have been so nice and why did he wait so long? How about his wife and children? Maybe she was imagining it all?

Not until after the police investigation, which revealed that Mr. Jackson had been picked up twice before on similar complaints, did Dana finally believe that she had almost been the victim of a rapist.

Most rapists do not conduct such long, intensive "interviews" with potential victims. Often the questioning lasts only a moment or two. Attackers interview you to see what kind of victim you will make, rather than to get specific information about you. If you talk, return their smile, and act glad to oblige some request, you fail the test. They assume you are a passive person who will trust them, or at least not expect danger, and will be startled enough to go along when they attack.

Our society, especially in the South and Midwest, fosters the attitude that you must be friendly to everyone. In an attempt to be pleasing, helpful, and friendly, teens often give a rapist a good "interview," only to become a victim of his attack a few minutes or hours later.

The following quiz should help you check up on your away-from-home safety. In each What if? situation, decide what you would do. Then read the correct, safest response to each situation.

WHAT WOULD YOU DO IF . . . ?

1. You are on a crowded elevator and your friend begins to discuss your plans for the day.
2. The elevator door opens and there is one unfamiliar man on it.
3. You need to buy something late at night.
4. Your club sponsors a door-to-door selling campaign and asks you to participate.
5. You walk by a male who whistles and makes a crude remark about your figure.
6. You are walking down the block and see a group of males standing idly on the sidewalk ahead.
7. You are walking along the street and a man moves his briefcase from in front of himself and exposes himself.
8. You are walking home and know a shortcut through a construction area.

9. You are shopping in the grocery store and a man asks you what time it is.
10. You are riding a bus and someone tries to talk to you or rubs up against you.
11. A man acts suspiciously toward you and a second man overhears and comes over to offer you help or to walk you home.
12. While you are walking, someone in a car pulls alongside you to ask directions. You cannot hear him very well.
13. You are hitchhiking and someone turns around and comes back to pick you up.
14. You are walking and you think someone is following you on foot.
15. You are walking and you think someone is following you in a car.
16. You are being followed and/or run off the road while driving.
17. Someone tries to get you to lower your window while you are stopped at a traffic signal.
18. You return to your car and it won't start. A man comes by and offers you help or a ride somewhere.
19. You are driving through the city late at night and have car trouble.
20. You are driving through the countryside away from other traffic late at night and you have car trouble.
21. Someone with car trouble tries to wave you down.
22. You return to your parked car and see someone in the back seat.
23. A child approaches you on a parking lot, tells you his uncle is having a heart attack, and asks you to drive him to the hospital.
24. You are asked to work overtime late at night in an empty building.
25. You are waiting to meet a friend in a restaurant. Some-

one comes over with a message that your friend has
been delayed and wants to meet you somewhere else.

26. Someone told you he lost his dog and wants you to help
him look for it.

27. You answer an ad in the paper from someone selling a
stereo and they want to take your name and phone
number and have someone else call you back later.

28. While you are driving alone, a car pulls up beside you
and the driver motions and points to your wheel as if
something is wrong with your car.

SAFEST RESPONSES

1. Shush the friend. Never discuss your plans in front of
strangers who may be pretending to not pay attention.
They may pick up clues as to where you might be at
what time, if you are carrying money or credit cards for
shopping, or when you will be alone later.

2. Don't get on. Elevators are common places of attack.
Pretend you forgot something and have to get it. Look
at your watch and say something like, "Oh, it's too late
now." Or, snap your fingers and mumble, "I forgot to
phone first."

If you are already on an elevator and a man gets on,
get off and wait for the next car. If, by some chance, you
cannot manage to get off before the door closes, stay
near the control buttons. Let him punch his floor first
and then you punch the button for an earlier floor. If
he makes a move to grab you, press the emergency
button and all the floor buttons you can hit.

If you want to go up, never get on an elevator that is
going down. Someone from the basement or parking

garage may have punched the button and be waiting to drag you off there. Wait until the elevator goes down to the basement and let it stop for you on the way back up to your floor.

3. Do without it or have someone go with you. Night errands are particularly dangerous because most rapes occur between 8:00 P.M. and 2:00 A.M. In a study done by Chappell and James among offenders at the Atascadero State Hospital, 96 percent of the rapists said they *always* checked to see if the intended victim was alone. The worst night to be out alone is a weekend night—Friday in particular. Weekends are rife with drinking rapists who have a paycheck and plenty of leisure time. If you must go out alone late at night, tell someone where you're going and when you'll be back.

4. Never go door-to-door on a selling project alone. Never go inside a home when invited. Always step back away from the door when talking to the customer. It is preferable to make your sales over the phone to people you know.

5. Pretend you do not hear him and keep walking. Some people have called such remarks "verbal rapes." On the surface, teens rarely see anything dangerous or derogatory about such comments. Our society teaches a female to be flattered when someone expresses appreciation for her looks. Some girls even base their self-esteem on how much attention they can attract from males.

However, a male's intentions with such remarks are rarely what the female perceives. First of all, such comments do not necessarily mean that the girl is attractive. Similar crude or obscene remarks are often made to very young children, as well as to the elderly and the unattractive. Researchers say that a girl who seems flattered by such remarks is much more likely to be attacked than one who pretends not to hear.

Second, a male's verbal rape frequently expresses hostility. He feels you have no right to be walking the street, to be out alone thinking you are just as safe and as good as he is. He builds his own ego strength by putting himself above you socially. Or he may be expressing hostility against someone he knows who resembles you. If he is of another race, he may be putting you down out of racial bitterness. Whatever the source of the hostility, such a verbal obscenity degrades and humiliates.

To respond to such remarks with boredom, annoyance, or contempt in an effort to destroy the man's macho self-image and make him feel stupid can be extremely dangerous. Such responses may make him feel that he has to "teach you a lesson," that you are not "too good" for him. Never make the man feel that you are superior to him by your tone of voice, eyes, or gestures. He may then grow even more hostile and determine to get even later.

Others respond to such verbal intimacies by looking away or looking frightened. As mentioned earlier, potential rapists are encouraged by someone who seems passive and fearful. If the remark was made directly and loudly to you, look alert and walk on by briskly.

The best way to handle such comments is to pretend you don't hear them. This is not the same as ignoring or pretending superiority. Dig around in your purse as if you are looking for something, look at a scrap of paper as if you were memorizing an errand list, check your watch and furrow your brow over a late appointment, look in the crowd of people across the street for your friend. Pretend to be preoccupied and pass quickly.

Verbal intimacies are not flattery: they are a put down, a humiliation. They are rooted either in hostility or in a view of you as an object for gratification. If you make the wrong response, such remarks are often followed by physical violence.

6. Cross the street or turn a corner and detour around them. Never walk through a group of males. They may make threatening remarks or try to detain you. The gang syndrome (which is discussed in Chapter 5) often drives males to try to prove their manhood to themselves or to the other members of the group.

7. Keep your face blank as if you didn't notice, keep walking, and report him to the police. Men who expose themselves to you are acting out the same domination impulse as the verbal rapist. They want to demonstrate their manhood by shocking and embarrassing you. Most psychologists agree that exhibitionists and "touchers" are harmless and will go no further. However, you should respond to them in the same way you respond to the verbal rapist.

8. Stay on the well-traveled path. Shortcuts may be full of places where rapists can hide and jump out to grab you without fear of passers-by.

9. Give him the time, if you have a watch, and cut short any further communication.

10. Refuse to talk. Chances are that in a conversation of any length at all, you may spill just the information he is looking for: whether you are alone, where you are going. Keep your plans to yourself.

Move closer to someone else and pretend you are with that person. Quietly ask the individual the time or directions to some place so that the "talker" will assume you know the person.

Always sit near the operator on public transportation. If someone tries to rub up against you or touch you, move away. If he persists and you know it was no accident, say in a loud voice, "Please keep your hands to yourself." This will embarrass him and alert others to the situation. If plenty of seats are available and a man sits next to you, be aware of his manner and intent. Find an excuse to get up and move. If you see the same thing happen to another girl on the bus or subway, move over and pretend to know her.

11. Refuse his help. Rapists often work in pairs. The first man may make obscene remarks or maybe just stare at you. The second man pretends to notice that you are in danger and acts the part of the big protector. He gains your grateful confidence and gets you to walk off with him. Later he is joined by the first man.

    If annoyed by someone, you choose the person to come to your rescue. Approaching anyone in uniform —a transportation operator, a store security guard, or anyone who looks official—will usually frighten an offender away. If necessary, ask a store clerk or another stranger for help.

12. Keep walking and tell him you don't know. Step back away from the car if you are stopped. Sometimes speaking softly is a ploy to get you to step close enough to the car to be pulled inside. Another common trick is for a rapist to drive along while you're waiting for a bus or a friend and ask directions. As a casual afterthought, he may offer you a ride. Or, he may take the directions, drive around a couple of blocks, and return saying he couldn't find the location and wants you to show him.

13. First of all, never hitchhike. If someone makes a special effort such as changing directions to pick you up, you know they have other plans in mind. Hitchhiking is the

most dangerous situation you can place yourself in. Teens, especially those caught up in the women's movement for freedom, often hitchhike out of a sense of independence and a challenge to beat the odds. Wanting to go where you please safely is a natural, admirable desire. But wishing for the right doesn't make it worth the risk. The average male knows it's dangerous and knows *you* know it's dangerous. He figures if you don't care that much about yourself, you won't mind the rape as payment for the ride. Hitchhiking is an invitation to rape.

Some girls feel that hitchhiking is safe as long as they are with a boyfriend or another male. This is not so. Never get in the car first. The driver may drive off before the friend has a chance to get in. Or he may force the companion out of the car somewhere down the road and take you on further.

14. Speed up. If the footsteps speed up, you know the person is following. Scream and run. Or stop and face the follower if you are in a crowded walkway. Stare him straight in the face. If he knows you have seen his face and could recognize him, he will usually keep walking right on past you.

Always walk curbside so you can't be pushed into an alley or building. If there are unlocked cars parked near the curb, jump inside, lock the doors, and honk the horn until your pursuer leaves. The last thing he wants is attention. If you are walking in a residential area, walk up to the first lighted house and shout, "Dad, open up, I'm home." Or just ring the doorbell and tell whoever answers that you are being followed. If they don't answer the door, scream "fire," and they will.

Vary your walking route and your time. Someone may watch you and know exactly what time you pass every day. Be aware of places along the way where you can stop and ask for help, for example, open businesses, or houses with lights always on. Always know exactly where you're going by checking a map before you leave.

Always walk briskly and look alert, as if you might run any moment. Someone who has an armful of packages or wanders slowly and aimlessly around is an easy target. She looks unaware, passive, and easy to catch off guard. Being alert, pushing packages in a cart or having a clerk from the store carry them out, and wearing shoes you can run in if you have to give you the edge when you have to scream and run at a moment's notice.

Researchers tell us that either screaming or running will deter half of all rapists. They are looking for an easy victim, one who will be immediately intimidated and will submit fearfully.

15. Turn around and walk in the opposite direction toward the approaching car. If it stops or turns around and the occupant calls to you, you know you are being followed. Scream and run.

16. Drive to the nearest police or fire station, where someone will be on duty at all hours, or drive to a business which you know is open. Don't drive home. The attacker will know where you live and may return for another visit; or, if no one happens to be home when you get there, the follower may attack you at your house when you get out of the car. If you can't find the police station or an open business, drive up on the sidewalk, honk the horn, screech your tires, drive from side to side—do anything to attract attention. Someone will report you to the police and they will come to your rescue. (However, always be sure it is the police before you stop. Some attackers blink their car lights or have some kind of flashing light rigged to imitate the police.

Police cars have flashing blue or red lights and will have the siren on. Keep driving until you are sure.)

If someone pulls up alongside you and then turns toward you in an attempt to run you off the road, throw your car into reverse, back up, and drive around him on the other side. If you cannot drive your car or get around him, stay inside and keep the engine running. He eventually will have to get out of his car to come and get you out of yours. When he walks toward you, drive toward him and run into him if you have to. It is either his injury or yours. Hitting him while going slowly, under fifteen miles per hour, will incapacitate him long enough for you to get away and call the police. Be sure to get his license number.

Always keep your car well tuned and full of gas, so you can drive wherever necessary to get help. If you often drive late at night alone, you may want to consider tricks others have suggested. Prop up a clothes basket, a tire, or a cardboard box with a hat or coat draped around it: someone following at a distance will think you have a passenger.

17. Do not, under any circumstances, open your window. If the man doesn't go away, honk your horn, or even drive through the stoplight. Never drive with windows down or doors unlocked. An attacker can easily sneak up while you are stopped and jump into the car.

18. Don't go with him or stand around while he tampers with your car. Often after a rapist sees you park your car and leave, he tampers with a few wires so it won't start. When you can't get it started later, he offers you a ride. If you don't go with him, he may pretend to repair it or actually repair it. After he gains your confidence, you lower the window to thank him. Then he forces you over, gets in, and drives you off somewhere. If someone

offers you assistance or works on your car, wait inside the car with the windows up. Talk through the window. If he doesn't get the car going, ask him to call the police for you. Don't go with him for help. If he lingers, begin honking the horn. To avoid attention, he will disappear.

19. Raise the hood, get back in the car, lock all the doors, and stay inside until someone comes along to offer help. When someone stops, don't get out of the car. Lower the window just enough to talk. Ask the person to call the police and tell them your location. Do not give anyone who stops your phone number to call your parents. He may save it for another occasion.

20. If you are away from frequent passers-by, you cannot stay in the car as if you were in the city. With no chance for an attacker to attract attention, he can break out your car windows. Most windows are shatterproof, but not unbreakable with a shoe or rock. Frederick Storaska, executive director of the National Organization for the Prevention of Rape and Assault, suggests that you raise the hood of your car, then hide somewhere off the road—behind a tree or in a ditch. Anyone who stops and looks at the car will not be able to see you in the dark and will think you have left the scene. Then you can choose who helps you. When a family or another woman comes along, you can come out from hiding and ask for assistance, or they can take you some place or call the police for you.

21. Don't stop. Keep driving until you can call the police and give them the stalled car's location. Often rapists use car trouble as a ploy. They wave on men who stop to offer help and wait for a female to stop so they can force her into their car or jump into hers.

22. Pretend you didn't see him and keep walking. If you pause, he may have time to get up and pull a gun or

knife on you. Go back to a store or a home and report the situation. Leave an article of men's clothing (a cap, shoe, or tie) on your car seat. Thinking you have a companion with you or that a man owns the car may deter someone from hiding in your car.

When you park and leave your car while it's still daylight, always park where there are lights. If you return after dark, the area will be well lighted. Write down if necessary exactly where you parked, so that you can go straight to your car. Always have your keys out in your hand. A pause to search your purse for the key gives an attacker time to sneak up on you. Always check the back seat of the car before getting in.

If you park in an attended garage or parking lot, never leave your house key on the car key ring. Never put your name or address on the key ring. Attendants can have copies of the key made while you are away, or they may sell house keys and addresses to someone else.

23. Don't drive him. Tell them that you will send help. Get to a phone and call an ambulance. It's a sad commentary on our society that you have to be suspicious of a plea for help and feel heartless. But pretending illness is also a common trick to get inside your car. The adult hires some child to approach your car and say that his "uncle" or "father" has just had a heart attack. When you come to see about the uncle or offer a ride, the adult tells the kid to go on. The child has made a little money and maybe goes on his way not knowing what he's been a party to. The "sick" uncle then forces you to drive him somewhere for the rape.

24. Don't accept the work if you will be alone in the building. Explain that you are afraid and ask that other employees be there also. Or, if you must work, get

permission for a parent or a friend to join you. The extra money is not worth the risk. Building attendants or vagrants may be watching for just such an opportunity.

Any deserted buildings are dangerous, libraries particularly. Don't study or wander off into the unlighted stacks. Someone may pull a knife and threaten you if you make any noise or force you to leave with him.

25. Do not take the message at face value. Check it out. Question him about the details; you may uncover some discrepancy. A rapist may be waiting at the new destination or on the way there. Stay where you are and get complete answers about the circumstances.

26. Make up an excuse why you cannot. This tearjerker is a common ploy to lure you into a path the attacker chooses or to gain your confidence so you get into a car with him. Who could resist feeling sorry for someone with a lost puppy?

27. Don't give out your name, number, or address. If you must think over the price or get in touch later about something, you take the seller's name and number and call him back. If you go to the seller's address to look over the stereo, always take someone with you.

28. Keep driving until you come to an open service station or until he gives up and passes you by. Convincing you that you have car trouble is another common trick. If you pull over, the rapist stops, pretends to examine your car a moment, and then pulls a knife and forces his way into your car.

Well, how did you do on your responses?

The biggest hesitation most will have in putting these precautions into practice is feeling that they might be mistaken and might embarrass someone or themselves. Or, you may hesitate to be hardhearted, but you may have to feel hardhearted for the sake of safety. Wishing our society were different doesn't make it so.

Sheryl, who was a victim of the "sick uncle" ploy, had this to say after her ordeal: "Now, if I have to be rude, I'm rude."

Remember that if you're attacked outdoors, your chances for escape are better than if you are attacked inside, where your screams cannot be heard.

When you scream, don't just yell "Help," "Leave me alone," or "Get away." People nearby may think you're having an argument with your boyfriend or father. Even if they realize that you're in trouble, they may not want to get involved. The 1964 case of New Yorker Kitty Genovese, who was murdered while numerous onlookers failed to respond to her screams, underscores the point that some people may not want to bother with your problem.

It's better to yell "Fire!" if you're attacked. People tend to respond out of a selfish motive for their own safety. Whatever you scream, scream loudly as you run away. The last thing an attacker wants is attention. A yelling, running female does tend to attract attention.

Take away-from-home safety seriously. Be alert to your surroundings and plan what you would do in any of the situations just described.

Above all, don't be embarrassed that you may have mistaken someone's intentions and embarrassed them or yourself. To be embarrassed is better than to be attacked.

CHAPTER **3**

Safety at Home

You've probably been warned to be home before dark ever since the first time you ventured out without your parents. Unfortunately, being home before dark is no guarantee you're safe.

Kelly, fifteen, sat at the kitchen table sewing one Saturday afternoon, trying to finish up a skirt to wear that night. Suddenly she felt a hand go over her mouth, and a man dragged her into the bedroom. Her five-year-old sister heard the scuffle and came shouting, "That's my sister!" Kelly yelled for her little sister to get help. But before the sister returned, the man raped her and fled.

As Kelly found out, home is no longer a secure place. Approximately one-third of all rapes take place in the victim's home. However, you can make yourself much safer if you are aware of rapists' "games" to get into your house or apartment building.

Read through the following quiz and consider how you would normally respond. Then compare your responses with the safest responses, which follow the quiz.

WHAT WOULD YOU DO IF . . . ?

1. The mailman brings a package to your door and says you have to sign for it.
2. A repairman comes to check the heating system.
3. Someone comes to your door claiming car trouble and wants to use your phone to call a garage.
4. Someone comes to your door and explains that he has driven a long way to see his uncle next door, who is not home. He wants to use your phone to call his uncle's work number or wait for a few minutes in your apartment to see if his uncle comes home.
5. Someone comes to the door, claiming to be a friend of your brother's and wanting to wait for him inside.
6. Someone calls "from your dad's office" and needs to talk to him. Your dad is not home.
7. Someone approaches the locked door of your apartment building at the same time you do. He can't find his key.
8. You hear someone breaking into your house.
9. You see someone sitting in a parked, unlighted car on your street.

TRUE OR FALSE?

1. If you're living in an apartment with only girls, use your first initial on the mailbox rather than your first name.
2. Chain locks and push-in-the-button locks are the securest kind.
3. If the apartment manager refuses to let you keep a dog, little can be done to change the situation.
4. Hiding a key outside your door or porch in case you get locked out is a good idea.

5.   When you go out, it is a good idea to leave just the outside light on to discourage attackers when you return.

SAFEST RESPONSES

1.   Ask the mailman to slip the paper under the door for you to sign. Have him leave the package outside, and pick it up after he leaves. If he says he can't get the paper under the door, have him come back to deliver the package later. Rapists have often posed as mailmen or delivery men. Although it is a little more trouble for the rapist, his wearing an official-looking uniform catches most girls off guard.

2.   Have the repairman slip his identification under the door to you while he waits outside. All repairmen have identification badges or cards. DeSalvo, the Boston Strangler, posed as a repairman to enter apartment after apartment. If for some reason the man doesn't have identification, ask for his company's name and number and phone to verify that he is supposed to be there. Or phone your parents at work to see if they are expecting someone. If the man is legitimate, then you can let him in and explain that you are sure he can understand your caution.

   Even if the repairman is legitimate, there is still no guarantee that he won't attack you if he thinks you are alone. Mention that someone else is in another part of the house, for example, "I hope the doorbell didn't wake my brother." Or if you're expecting a repairman and will be home alone, invite a friend over while he's there.

3.   Say that your dad is using the phone now. Ask whom he

wants to call and say you'll make the call for him when your father is off the phone. If he says he doesn't know the number, tell him you'll check the Yellow Pages for him. Claiming injury, sickness, or car trouble is a common way for rapists to play on your sympathies and get into your house.

4.   Don't let him in. Say you have other company or that your family is in a heated discussion at the moment, or that you're waiting for a phone call and may have to leave in a few minutes.

This is also a common line for rapists who play on your desire to be helpful to your next-door neighbor.

5.   Tell him your brother isn't home or can't come to the door now and that he'll have to come back later. Don't let him come in to wait. If you think the visitor might be legitimate and he keeps hanging around outside, phone another of your brother's friends to ask if he recognizes the visitor's name.

6.   Don't tell him your dad isn't home. Say he can't come to the phone at the moment. Take the caller's name and number and say that your dad will phone him as soon as possible.

Never tell any caller you are home alone. If your parents are going out, be sure to ask if they are expecting any calls. Rapists often claim to be someone from work or someone who wants to come over and give you a gift or free lessons if you can answer a particular question.

Some girls assume the caller is legitimate if he knows the family name or her first name. In our society, getting someone's name is not difficult. Rapists get names and addresses from key rings, lost billfold IDs, mailboxes, ads on public bulletin boards, newspaper write-ups, work or school directories, as well as from unsuspecting neighbors or an earlier wrong number call.

A wrong number should be handled as follows:

CALLER: May I speak to Eddie?
YOU: You have the wrong number.
CALLER: Who is this?
YOU: What number were you dialing?
CALLER: 926-2721
YOU: You misdialed.
                or
YOU: That's my number, but there's no one here by that name.

          If the caller persists, hang up.

Knowing your name is no guarantee that a caller really knows you or a family member.

Obscene calls have a different motivation. Rather than trying to find out if you're home alone, obscene callers get their thrills by hearing your voice and reaction. Sometimes a caller will only breathe heavily into the receiver and say nothing, or he may say vulgar things. He may pretend to be taking a sex survey for some agency and may want you to answer some questions. (Such surveys are never taken over the phone.)

Another caller may just want to talk to you without giving his name, pretending you are someone he knows. Such callers get their kicks from their imagination. They may be imagining what you look like and just want to hear a woman's voice. Others get their thrills by upsetting you, hearing the shock or anger in your voice.

The best way to handle such calls is simply to get off the phone. Don't antagonize the caller by blowing a loud whistle in his ear or talking back. If he got your number from the phone book, he can also get your address from the same place. Simply hang up without answering his comments. Otherwise, you may be reacting just as he wants you to, and he may continue to call back.

Report all such calls to the police, especially if they involve a specific gimmick or line. The police can check call patterns, and they often put notices in the paper or on television to warn others about such calls.

For repetitive callers: Tap the receiver lightly with your fingernail or a pencil in a steady rhythm to imitate the sound of tracing equipment. Or direct a comment away from the receiver but loud enough to be heard: "That's him, trace it."

7. Wait until he finds his key and unlocks the door for himself, gets buzzed in, or leaves. Otherwise, leave and call the superintendent or your parents and ask them to come to the door. Pretending to have lost a key or nonchalantly approaching the door at the same time another resident does is another easy way strangers get into apartment buildings.

8. Keep your head. Try not to freeze in position. If he is coming in one door, go out the opposite door and run to a neighbor's house to call the police. Know your way around your house in the dark; practice moving quickly from room to room when the lights are out. Note furniture that may be in your path.

    If you have only one door, phone the police (always have emergency numbers posted on all phones). If the police don't answer immediately, dial the operator and give her the message and your address. Then run to a room that has a door which can be locked. Even a weakly locked door may stall the attacker until help arrives.

Sometimes an attacker keeps a victim captive in her house or apartment for several hours. Make a point to get to know your neighbors. Know which ones are home at what time of day. Perhaps you can arrange some kind of code with your neighbor to signal trouble. You might arrange to set an empty bottle outside the door or pull open an habitually closed shade to signal for help. If you know neighbors are home to hear, make lots of noise—scoot furniture around, play the record player unusually loud, turn it up and down several times. If your captor asks what you're doing, tell him that you're nervous and want to take your mind off things.

If you are raped, don't let the rapist escape without trying to get something to identify him by. If at all possible, get to a window to see if you can see his car and get a license number. Kelly, the girl mentioned at the beginning of the chapter, grabbed a robe and followed her attacker outside to get his license number as he drove away. He was later convicted and sentenced to twenty years.

Be alert when you return home. Let whoever drove you home come in or wait outside while you check around to see that everything's okay. Make noise when you return to let anyone hiding inside have a chance to get out.

Trust your feelings. If you come in and things "just don't feel right," get out. Go next door and ask a neighbor to come back with you. It's better to be wrong and embarrassed than right and raped. It might be a good idea to leave a "plant" when you go out. Place a newspaper or some other object in a strange position where it might be disturbed. Check that item when you walk into the house.

9. Watch for a few minutes to see what is going on. Chances are that if someone is parked in an unlighted car for as long as an hour, he is not just waiting for a friend. Call the police to report it. They welcome such calls and need your help in checking out suspicious incidents and people.

    Be alert to strange people in the area, particularly salesmen going door to door. Watch to see if they check door handles when no one answers the door. They are looking for an unlocked door; report them.

    Never give out your neighbor's name or schedule. The attacker may intend either to wait until the person is home, or to phone, using her name as if he knew her. Always be leery and pretend ignorance about your neighbors.

TRUE-OR-FALSE RESPONSES

1. False. If you are living alone or with other girls in an apartment, don't advertise the fact on your mailbox. By now, attackers know about the advice to use one initial instead of a first name if you are a girl alone. Use your first two initials, as men often do.

2. False. Doors with press-in-the-button locks or chain locks are the very worse kind. Button locks can be opened with a slim, hard object like a credit card. Chain locks can be snapped with one good blow. Make sure you have a deadbolt or dropbolt lock fastened securely to both the door and door facing.

    And use them! Most people have locks on their doors. The trouble is that they don't use them. Lock up even when you are home, and always when you leave, even if it's just for a few minutes to go next door, to the mailbox, or to the laundry room. Keep the garage locked also. Attackers often hide in unlocked, unlighted garages and catch the victim before she reaches the house.

3. False. Many cities have ordinances that say a manager cannot prohibit tenants from keeping a dog for protection. Check by calling city hall. A dog is a girl's best friend. If your landlord or parents object, sell them on the idea of safety. If all else fails, post a "Beware dog" sign outside anyway.

4. False. Any attacker knows to check the flowerpot by the door, the mailbox, or the welcome mat. If you want to make sure you don't accidentally lock yourself out, give a key to a neighbor who is generally home.

5. False. Never leave only your outside light on. That advertises that you are away from home. Leave lights on inside your house to discourage intruders. Also leave a radio or television playing. If the entryway, hallway, street, apartment building, or parking area is not well lighted, get other tenants to sign petitions to get adequate lighting installed.

How did you do on home safety? If, after taking the true-or-false quiz, you are still unsure about the security of your house or apartment, have the police give you a free check of the premises for advice on safety measures. If your parents are too busy to take these recommended precautions after you point them out, get a do-it-yourself book from the library, invite a friend to help, and take the project on yourself.

If you found "lines" in the "What if?" section which could have worked on you, double-check the correct response so you can use it when necessary. Remember, the attacker is looking for a naive, friendly, passive victim. Don't let him con you to get through your front door.

CHAPTER 4

Safety in Social Situations

Getting ready for a date, planning for a party, visiting an old family friend, accepting a baby-sitting job—these are hardly times when you consider the danger of rape. However, Frederick Storaska of the National Organization for the Prevention of Rape and Assault finds that about 35 percent of all rapes are committed by a date or in a dating environment. Another 35 percent are committed by acquaintances such as neighbors, relatives, bosses, friends of friends, and so forth.

In other words, two out of three rapes occur in what could be called social situations. It's not always strangers who catch you off guard; you are generally leery of them. Knowing someone often blinds you to his intentions, makes it more difficult to handle an attack verbally, and complicates reporting the incident to the police.

Many date rapes occur in situations similar to this one experienced by Rhonda, age seventeen.

Terri, Rhonda's best friend, invited her over one Friday night to meet Brian, a college friend who had come home with her brother for the weekend. Rhonda jumped at the opportunity because Terri had made him sound so attractive. The evening went well. Terri, her brother Mark, the college friend Brian, and Rhonda stayed around the house and listened to records and later in the evening went out for hamburgers.

Brian called Rhonda the next morning and asked if she would like to go to a football play-off game that Saturday night. He explained that Terri and Mark had to go with their parents to a special dinner, but would be home by the time the game was over and would meet them afterward.

Rhonda accepted the date, and they enjoyed the game. Afterward, she and Brian drove to Terri's and found that the family was still not home. Brian pulled a key out of his pocket so they could go inside and wait. Rhonda was hesitant and at first suggested that they just wait a few minutes in the car until her friend came home. Brian told her it was too cold, and he didn't want to waste the gas to keep the heater running. Then he made some remark about how he forgot how "naive and sheltered" high school girls were. Rhonda looked embarrassed and didn't know what to say. After all, he was Mark's best friend. Mark trusted him or his parents wouldn't have left Brian with a house key to come and go as he pleased. What would they think about her when Brian told them she was too scared to go into the house with him?

Rhonda agreed and they went inside. Brian walked through the house looking in all the rooms, then came back into the kitchen. Rhonda thought of calling her mother to let her know where she was. When she mentioned it, Brian grinned, rolled his eyes upward, and pointed to the phone. She picked up the receiver and then decided against it. If she told her mother she was in someone's house alone, her mother would tell her to come right home. Besides, what could she say with Brian standing right by the phone?

Brian wandered back to Mark's room to put on the stereo. Rhonda waited in the den. Brian kept mumbling something to her about which records she would like to hear. After asking him several times to repeat what he'd said, she walked down the hall into Mark's room. Brian closed the door behind her, kissed her, and then pushed her onto the bed. She struggled to get up, telling him she wanted to go home. He began to pull off her clothes, laughing at her. When she said she was going to tell what happened, he continued to taunt her, "You came into the house of your own free will, didn't you? If you didn't want it, why didn't you call your mother a while ago? Why did you follow me back here? Who's going to believe you didn't agree to it? Tell me that!"

Rhonda kept struggling to get away, but she was unsuccessful. Brian raped her, then ordered her to dress, and drove her home.

Date rapes like Rhonda's happen every day. It's very difficult to say just where, when, and how Rhonda could have avoided the incident, to see where she could have picked up the clues and called a halt to the situation without being embarrassed herself, or embarrassing an "innocent" date.

She had been introduced to Brian through trusted friends. She had no way of knowing that Terri and Mark wouldn't be home as they had said they would be. She certainly couldn't be faulted for not sitting in a cold car. Phoning her mother would have surely brought a lecture and ended what she had thought would be a pleasant evening.

Looking back to the incident, Rhonda feels very stupid and guilty about going inside with Brian. Of course, she was not really at fault for the rape; Brian was responsible for his own behavior. But her parents blame her for the attack since she went into the house with him.

Victims of other crimes, for instance, people who are robbed, are seldom blamed for being careless. They may blame themselves for leaving the door unlocked, but others don't blame them for the robbery. Likewise, a victim shouldn't blame herself for not being cautious enough about a rape situation. All she can do is learn for the future.

Let's rethink Rhonda's situation and see exactly how she got into the predicament and what she might have done differently.

First of all, she trusted someone who was untrustworthy, an understandable occurrence. We often treat people who are almost strangers as friends because we transfer our trust from the known friend to the new acquaintance. We rest our judgment on the mutual friend's judgment. But sometimes the friend's judgment is wrong or naive. The days of a lengthy, chaperoned introduction are long gone; everyone passes trust from an old friend to a new one.

Rule # 1 from Rhonda's experience: Be careful whom you date, how well you know the person, and whose judgment you're trusting.

Second, Rhonda let Brian arrange all the details for the date, another understandable situation. He had explained that Terri and Mark would return after the banquet and be home when they returned from the game. Rhonda never thought to call Terri and make sure of their plans.

Rule # 2 from Rhonda's experience: Don't let your date make all the arrangements and accommodations, especially if any part of the arrangements give you cause for concern.

Don't accept dates for secluded spots with someone you don't know very well—picnics by the lake, meeting at someone's apartment, unchaperoned parties.

If you know there will be alcohol and other drugs present, you are walking into a particularly dangerous situation. While neither liquor or marijuana is a sexual turn-on, both drugs bolster a male's ego, make him a little bolder, reduce his judgment about getting caught, and encourage his anything-goes attitude. Peer pressure to join in the "fun" may be something more than you want to handle. You may be tempted to tackle the unusual circumstances out of a spirit of adventure, rebellion, curiosity, or over-confidence. However strong the temptation to accept the date arrangements, don't.

Double-check all arrangements that involve overnight accommodations or out-of-town trips. Think up a good excuse to call someone you know well and check the details. Let him or her know your plans and what your date told you —before you go.

Third, Rhonda and Brian had a communication problem. Brian may have known his friends would not be back until late and may have set the whole thing up. In this particular incident, Terri and Mark had actually planned to return after the game, just not quite as early as Brian had said they would.

Brian didn't consider his attack a rape. Since Rhonda had kissed him several times earlier in the evening, had agreed to go into the house alone with him, and hadn't called her mother, he believed or rationalized that she really was as anxious for the sexual encounter as he.

On the other hand, Rhonda thought she knew Brian well because they had been together the evening before. She meant nothing by returning his earlier kisses; she went inside the house to avoid saying she didn't trust him; and she didn't call her mother because she didn't want to worry her, didn't want to have to go home, and didn't want Brian to think she was a child.

They didn't communicate.

Rule # 3 from Rhonda's experience: Communicate your feelings, intentions, and limits early in the date. Understand the difference between the signals you are sending and how your date may interpret them.

This rule is a tall order. People of all ages and in all kinds of situations and relationships have trouble communicating.

Consider for a moment what signals a girl may send out and how she may feel about those signals. A girl is trained to be pleased when a male makes a pass at her. Gloria Steinem calls this the "man junkie" syndrome, the need to gain self-esteem from being thought attractive or desirable by the opposite sex.

A girl may inadvertently tease by the way she sits, stands, walks, dresses, smiles, talks, jokes, hugs, and kisses "just friends." Once she knows that the boy finds her attractive, she is satisfied. The game is over—for the girl, but not necessarily for the boy. He does not always understand that the girl's flirting is just a game, that she means to go no further. Certainly, he should understand and respect her wishes when she calls a halt, but he doesn't always. Instead, he often feels resentful and tricked.

What a boy may perceive as teasing and a come-on may not be meant that way at all. A girl may be quite unaware of signals a boy may be interpreting. Either way—with the intent to tease or not—there's a communication problem.

A boy may read signals incorrectly *or pick up signals when they don't exist.* He, too, has been conditioned by society to act in a certain way toward females. He is told that girls don't always mean "no" when they say it. He learns that "no" may be a face-saving ploy when a girl really means "maybe," "I'll think about it," or even "yes." He may assume that if she makes a remark with sexual overtones or is affectionate with many people, she is free with her sexual favors. He may even think that the girl *expects* an advance from him, that all males are supposed to be super go-getters on dates, and that she will think him strange if he doesn't try something. Whenever he does make a pass, he is putting his ego out for her to see—and hurt. He will defend it to the utmost.

Finally, a date may even have the ridiculous idea that the girl should pay him for the date with sex. Certainly no girl really prices herself that low, but some males may expect it.

Whatever the boy perceives about how you feel, you must communicate your feelings from the outset to be safe and to control the situation. Accepting a date to a lonely, secluded spot or failing to even ask where you're going may make a boy think that your intentions are the same as his.

Don't be embarrassed to say that you can't go to such and such a place. Say that your parents won't permit it or that you simply don't want to go. Tell him how you feel about the situation immediately, but do try to save his ego. Communicate that you are not rejecting him, but that these are your limits with all males. By allowing him to save face, you can help minimize his feelings of personal rejection.

Most date rapes are not the "mis-communication" type at all. In most cases, the boy plans the situation from the very beginning and knows that you will object. He goes to great lengths to handle all the details. In such a case, you are left to escape as best you can. You can pretend that you are going along with him but that you want to use some birth control protection. Then talk him into taking you to a store where you can phone your parents or simply wait inside until help arrives.

You can pretend that you are afraid you will get caught and suggest that you go to another location. On the way, look for a chance to escape or get to a phone. If neither of these suggestions works, resist as discussed in Chapters 6 and 7.

Remember, to prevent rape in dating situations, be sure you:

- Choose your date carefully. Ask around about him. Don't immediately transfer your trust from an old friend to a new one.
- Control the environment. Choose the dating activity and the place.
- Stay away from places where there will be alcohol and drugs.
- Communicate your intentions and limitations early.
- Try to protect your date's ego.
- Always carry money for a "rescue" phone call.

One last warning about the date rape situation. Your date may not be the attacker himself but may put you in danger by parking in a deserted area. Rapists often roam favorite parking spots to attack couples. If you insist on parking with your boyfriend, always park with the car headed outward. Never lower the windows enough for someone to reach in and unlock the doors. Always keep the key in the ignition. If your boyfriend is pulled out of the car first, drive away if you can and get help. You can't help by staying. The rapist is after you; he will let your date go if you escape. The best advice is to do your "parking" in your own home with your parents in the next room.

Let's consider another dangerous social situation—an attack by a friend of the family, the boss, or a relative. This acquaintance rape, like the date rape, is much more complicated than the stranger rape. This rapist leaves you feeling betrayed because you trusted him, feeling guilty because you didn't recognize the danger and do something about it earlier, and feeling confused about whether and whom to tell.

Ginger, fourteen, knew Barney and his family quite well. He had children only a few years older than she, and he worked with her dad. Barney considered himself a ladies' man; his pats and hugs were expected and excused among their social circle.

Both Ginger's dad and Barney had decided to run for positions on the school board. Over the weeks during the campaigning, tension built up between Ginger's father and Barney; much of the earlier socializing stopped. Ginger tried to stay out of the election difficulties, sure that things would be back to normal after the voting. She continued to speak to Barney and act as if there were no political race in the background. She even called his wife to sell them tickets to the sophomore spaghetti dinner at school.

The night of the dinner, Barney was his usual, jovial, flirtatious self. While the after-dinner talent show was going on, a few of the students, Ginger among them, had KP duty in the homemaking department. Barney left the talent show audience and wandered back into the kitchen area. He made small talk for a few minutes with the three kids washing and drying dishes, and then followed Ginger into the adjoining cafeteria, where she was rolling up the paper tablecloths. He caught her arm as she passed the doorway to a supply closet and pulled her inside. He forced her up against him and covered her mouth with his. At first, Ginger was startled and speechless. She couldn't believe it was actually happening—not Barney, not a friend of theirs, not with his wife Sharon sitting out in the audience. She struggled as he yanked at her clothes, and she finally pulled away and ran crying from the closet. She ran back to the kitchen, and safely inside, leaned against the wall, still crying.

A friend came over and pulled Ginger back outside into the hallway to find out what had happened. It was all Ginger could do to get the story out about Barney. What could she do? How was she going to face him? What would her dad do when he found out?

He'd be angry enough to kill Barney. At the least, he would want to bring charges against him—there would be a big scandal. Some people might even think she and her dad had made up the story to win the school board election. After all, Barney didn't complete the rape; there was no evidence. It was just her word against his.

After a long, tearful discussion, Ginger and her friend concluded that Ginger couldn't do anything but try to forget the whole situation, to act as if nothing had happened, and to stay away from Barney.

That's what Ginger did. Barney acted as though nothing

had ever happened and smiled and flirted in her presence as if it had only been a game. (He won the election.)

Ginger still thinks that maybe she did the wrong thing by keeping quiet, but how does anyone ever know what's best?

What should you do if you find yourself in a similar predicament?

First, try to recognize danger signals from a potential acquaintance rapist. Such signals include his staring at you strangely and often; looking you over; frequently touching and patting you; "playfully" tousling or tickling you; commenting about how you are "developing" or how maturely you behave or dress; telling sexual jokes in your presence; bringing up the subject of sex in other ways; maneuvering you into situations where you are often alone together.

If you are aware of any of these signals, communicate your feelings clearly. Look alert, be suspicious, act annoyed if you catch him staring at you. Move away when he touches you, even if he does it in a "playful" mood. Discourage talk about sexual topics, leave the room if necessary. Stay where there are other people. Make an excuse not to go with him when he invites you somewhere alone.

If he has no ulterior motives, he will not notice or be offended by such turn-offs. If he has such motives, you don't care whether he's offended or not.

If the potential offender does carry through and attack you, tell someone. Often the situation can be handled with minimal involvement of other family members or friends. The fear that you might embarrass or upset the social situation is minor considering the offense and the chance of a repeat.

Tell whoever you feel is most likely to react in an objective way and will be able to ensure your future safety.

Baby-sitting is a third potentially dangerous social situation. Sitters are often lured away from home when someone calls from a phone booth and asks her to babysit. When she leaves the house or arrives at the address, the rapist attacks. At other times, "friends" of the people for whom you're baby-sitting may call or come over and take advantage of your situation. Sometimes, you may have trouble with fathers who drive you home after baby-sitting.

Here are some good baby-sitting rules to follow:

1. If you must accept baby-sitting jobs from people you don't know, get their number and phone them back later in the day. Pretend to be a saleswoman and ask if they would be interested in buying photos for their children. Or claim you forgot the time they need you to come or ask what time they'll be home so you can let your mother know what time to expect you. If the person who answers doesn't know what you're talking about, be leery. Call back and refuse the job.

   If the baby-sitter request comes from someone who seems legitimate, ask around about him and his family in the neighborhood.

2. Don't let a first-time employer pick you up. Have a parent or a friend drive you over. He will know that others know where you are and can identify him.

3. When the parents leave, ask if they are expecting any calls or any friends to come over. If so, take the names and numbers. If someone else comes over, don't answer the door. If someone calls, tell him that his friends can't come to the phone and will return the call later. Never let anyone know you are there alone. Find out before the parents leave which neighbors they know and whom you can call for help.

4. Call your parents before you start home from the baby-sitting job. They will know to look for you if you are not home in a reasonable time.
5. If a father drives you home and attacks, play on his sympathy. Use one of the defenses mentioned in Chapter 6. Get him to see you as a human being; remind him of his little daughter who will babysit some day.

Again, even in social situations—dating, friend and family gatherings, baby-sitting jobs—rape is a real threat. Depending on which research statistics you have at hand, from 35 percent to 75 percent of all rapes are by people you know.

Be alert to warning signs. Communicate your feelings early and take control of the situation.

PART TWO

During an Attack— Fighting Back

CHAPTER **5**

Understanding What Makes the Rapist Rape

You may be asking, "Why do I want to understand the rapist?" If he humilates, degrades, injures, and even kills victims, why should I want to understand him?

Primarily, you need to understand a rapist to defend yourself. You need to learn what kind of men rape, recognize their signals, and know how to react to different rapists once attacked. Your ability to talk an attacker out of the rape depends a great deal on your being able to "read" his motivations. (More about defenses to particular types of rapists in Chapters 6 and 7.)

Second, you need to understand the rapist to be able to change society, at least your small corner of society. We'll discuss popular attitudes that contribute to making such men menaces.

In a Harris public opinion poll in 1977, 87 percent of Americans believed that only sick, perverted men rape.

Perhaps that's why girls and women are so often taken by surprise by the acquaintance rapist or the "normal"-looking male. They are assuming that since only psychotics rape, they will see overt warning signals about a man's potential for such violence.

Without studying and researching the nature of rapists, the average female's concept of an attacker is something akin to this:

- probably of another race
- an older man
- sexually deprived, unmarried

Statistics say otherwise.

- Rapists almost always attack females of their own race.
- The vast majority of rapists are between fifteen and twenty-four years old.
- Forty-three percent are married.
- Most rape from hate, not sexual attraction.
- Fifty-eight percent of single rapes are planned.
- Ninety percent of group rapes are planned.
- Attackers choose the place and rape whoever happens along.

This picture of the average rapist comes from FBI reports and numerous independent studies of police records and interviews with convicted rapists. These studies give us concrete statistics and also a much broader picture of the rapist as an individual.

Let's look at some rapists' motivations.

HATE RAPIST

This attacker has a deep hatred of women, primarily resulting from his relationship with his mother, his wife, or even his father. His mother may have been domineering and perhaps wouldn't let him decide anything for himself or express his feelings. The mother may have been the head of the family, forcing the rapist and his father into a subordinate existence over a long time. The man has built up a deep resentment toward her which he never can express to her verbally. Instead, he directs that hatred to all women, whom he sees as trying to dominate him, do him in, suffocate him.

Perhaps the mother was not particularly domineering, but was unaffectionate. She stopped hugging, kissing, and showing interest in him; she ignored him when he very much needed her love and attention. Again, because he was unable to get affection from her, he has become hostile toward her and all women.

From his father, the rapist may have picked up the idea that women are cruel, inferior, and manipulative. In other words, the father despises women and has passed this bitterness along to his son.

Another source of a rapist's hatred may be his relationship with his wife. The rapist may feel that she is too domineering, that she completely runs their financial and social life. If he is weak and can't stand up to her, he buries the hostility when around her but takes it out on other women.

The hatred-motivated rape is an attempt to put women in their place and to show contempt. Rapists with this motivation are often more violent. A struggle from the victim may excite them more and give them the pleasure of revenge.

This type of rapist doesn't give out warning signs because of the very nature of his motives. He will not openly show hatred and hostility toward his wife or parents. He can't. He has suffered in silence; that's why he rapes to get even. He may be nice-looking, polished, socially acceptable, detached, seemingly always the gentleman under perfect control.

EGO-HELP RAPIST

This rapist needs help with his self-image. He often has a low IQ and lives a dead-end existence. He has few goals, a low-paying job, little education, no hobbies. He is frustrated over who he is and where he's going.

Officer H. C. Meell, of the Houston Police Department, says, "He imagines she [the victim] is up on a pedestal, looking down on him." He feels he must "teach the victim a lesson."

In addition to external circumstances' increasing the rapist's low self-esteem, this attacker may have internal confusions about his role as a man. He may have lacked a strong male role model when he was growing up. If he saw his father as a weak, ineffective husband and father, he may feel that he is just as weak and passive. He then has to prove himself.

Often he has strong homosexual tendencies and wishes to cover them up by proving his manhood through rape. In researchers Groth and Burgess's interviews with rapists, over one-third of them admitted that they couldn't even complete the sex act during the assault.

Giving further clues about his lack of self-esteem and wanting to prove to himself that he is a man, a rapist often comments about his sexual skill to his victims. He makes statements like, "Aren't you enjoying this? All my victims like this." Some rapists even delude themselves about the victim's reaction to the point where they try to make a date to see her again. (Some victims have gone along with this and have had the police waiting at the "date.")

Rapists with this type of motivation may be either brutal and violent or sympathetic and considerate of the victim. Those who are attempting to raise themselves (to prove that they are economically, socially, or mentally as good as the woman) beat and bruise her during the attack. They want to impress her with their strength and their ability to dominate her. On the other hand, this rapist may show consideration and sympathy in an attempt to get his victim to "love" him and build his esteem. The irony of such cases stands out.

A thirteen-year-old was walking home from a basketball game one night, when two men drove up beside her and pulled her into their truck. On the way out of town to a secluded spot for the rape, the girl complained that she had to go to the bathroom. The men pulled off the road and let her out. When she said that she was embarrassed and couldn't go with them watching, they turned their heads and walked up the road a piece to give her privacy.

Another victim, age seventeen, was abducted from her apartment parking lot by an armed rapist. After he had stripped her and she complained of being cold, he took off his jacket and gave it to her. He rolled the sweater he wore into a pillow for her head. After the rape, the man asked her where she wanted to be taken. When she named a nearby grocery, he drove her there to let her out. When she started to walk away, he handed her two quarters. "For the phone," he said. "I gave you an extra one in case you lose the first one in a phone that doesn't work."

Both the violent and the "sympathetic" rapist with the ego-help motivation rapes essentially to say, "Notice me, love me. I am a man."

TAKE-THE-OPPORTUNITY RAPIST

This rapist moves with the circumstances. He does not set out to rape, either out of hate or low self-esteem. He rapes on impulse. He intends only to rob the apartment; but when the victim comes home from school and catches him, he takes the opportunity.

Often, acquaintance rapes fall into this category. The rapist and victim are thrown together alone. No one else is in the house. He puts his natural defenses against such impulses in a hold pattern and attacks while he has the chance, before even thinking of the later consequences of their social situation.

One opportunist rapist says, "I was just driving along at the edge of the park, minding my own business, thinking about nothing in particular. I'd been drinking a little, but just minding my own business. And there she was, this girl just walking along out of the park. Nobody was around. She was too . . . convenient."

The opportunist rapist often divides women into two

categories. Some women are respectable. He sees them as people—mothers, sisters, girlfriends. He wouldn't think of raping them. The other category of women he sees as objects—nobodies with few or no morals. He lumps hitchhikers, runaways, prostitutes, and girls who frequent bars into this "object" category. If he gets the opportunity, raping them doesn't matter.

DRUNK RAPIST

The category of drunk rapists overlaps the other motivational categories above, but I want to discuss this type separately because the Kinsey Institute for Sex Research finds that 39 percent of all rapists have been drinking before committing rape. Drinking lowers a man's natural defenses against illogical impulses. Under the influence of alcohol, he sheds his inhibitions, becomes bolder, and develops a devil-may-care attitude.

Such rapes often take place in a social situation where the victim and rapist know each other.

PSYCHOTIC RAPIST

The psychotic attacker has lost touch with reality. Something inside his brain has snapped. Imagining a slur directed toward him or seeing a particular incident or object may set him on a violent path and trigger the rape. Few rapists actually fall into this category.

INTELLECTUAL RAPIST

Eldridge Cleaver claims this motivation/rationalization. He says he raped white women as revenge for the whites' treatment of blacks. Sometimes terrorist groups claim to rape hostages for political revenge and as a call to political action.

GROUP or GANG RAPISTS

Different studies show that gang or group rape accounts for from 18.5 percent to 43 percent of all rapes. Although individual members may fall into some of the categories above, the group as a unit functions from an altogether different motivation.

Teenage girls are often the victims of these group rapes due to their social life-style. Their activities take them to common meeting grounds with groups of teenage boys.

These boys are often not in formally organized gangs but are groups who just happen to be together. They may happen to leave a party together and cruise around looking for something to top off the evening. They may take off from college or work together for the weekend and decide to drive across the state. They may meet at a movie or pool hall and link up for the evening. Finally, some may be members of a highly organized gang with a definite leader and a social hierarchy.

Regardless of how and why groups get together, members generally have several things in common: They are weak and insecure about their own values, personality, and masculinity. They desperately need peer approval. They give each other permission to be big men and set up some daring criteria for each one to prove his worth.

Because of the reasons behind group rapes, these rapists do not choose a victim. Rather, they choose a method and a place. Amir says that 90 percent of group rapes are planned; they do not just happen because an attractive girl walks by. The group chooses a place to take a victim—usually away from possible interruptions—and then drives around trying to find someone alone. At other times, members may station themselves in a secluded spot and catch whoever happens by.

Not all members of the group participate with the same willingness. Some participate aggressively. They are the leaders; after having proved their masculinity, they encourage the others. Other members participate because they can't stand up to peer pressure or are afraid they'll be laughed at, hurt, or kicked out of the group if they don't go along with the dare.

Together, the group rapists attack to prove something to themselves and to each other. What the other group members think becomes the strongest motivation of its individual members.

To fully understand what makes the rapist tick, however, you also have to look beyond these inner deficiencies. Society subtly suggests rape to all males.

How?

First, consider the idea that men are the stronger sex—dominant, supreme. Remember, a constitutional amendment was needed to even give women the right to vote. Men have traditionally run the government and civilization and been the decision-makers. Women have traditionally been property—to love or to exploit. In war, the victor got the spoils, including conquered women. Men are taught to compete for women and to win them as prizes—for example, to get to kiss the homecoming queen. The decision about how to treat the prize—to please or to humiliate— is the man's.

The idea that women are weaker and easily dominated against their will (whether true or untrue) has given men the courage to try to intimidate. If they can't subdue and frighten by sheer size or strength, they can always find a knife or a gun.

Men are conditioned to be tough and to use force when necessary to get what they want. Women, on the other hand, are told that strength is unfeminine. They are not trained in sports or other competition to be strong and aggressive. They are taught that because they are physically weaker, they couldn't possibly overpower a male attacker.

Besides society's conditioning that men are stronger and supreme and that women are weak and are their property, society bombards males with sexual ideas through pornography. Susan Brownmiller writes, "Pornography . . . is . . . designed to dehumanize women, to reduce the female to an object of sexual access." Others have said pornography causes a "fast-food" attitude towards sex. Furthermore, law officials across the country say that their experience with offenders who are caught with pornographic materials in their possession leads these officials to believe that such materials motivate sex crimes.

Despite all the evidence to the contrary, some people argue that pornography is actually good for society. They contend that all of the male's sexual energy will be drained by looking at so much pornography. Therefore, males don't need to actually attack women. Dr. John Drakeford refutes that idea by pointing out that that's what many have said about violence on television. According to this theory, if people see enough violence on television, they won't need to act out their own hostility. That theory has come into disrepute as violence continues to permeate our entire society.

Others argue that if a person is constantly exposed to sex through pornography, he will gradually become dulled and lose interest in the idea. The growing market for pornographic magazines and the welcome audiences for pornographic films certainly refute the idea that males are losing interest in such materials. What do your own ears on your school campus tell you about males' losing interest in pornography?

Finally, some people argue that pornography has no effect whatsoever on sexual attacks. If what our minds are bombarded with in books, magazines, and movies has no effect, then businessmen have certainly wasted a lot of advertising dollars over the years! Soft-drink advertisers tell us that a certain drink adds zest to our life. We believe it and sales grow. Hair product companies tell us that their shampoo makes hair shinier. We believe that and sales grow. Campaigns on physical fitness have half the population jogging around the neighborhood every morning.

By examining any of the evidence, common sense dictates that when males are continually bombarded with sexual stimuli, it does have some effect. So when sex is used either overtly or subtly in advertising, the message is likely to be believed just as readily. But we really don't have to depend on common sense. Police officers and rapists themselves often say that their ideas came from current issues of pornographic magazines or movies.

Whether pornography influences "normal" men to rape or just pushes "abnormal" ones over the edge, it still plays a big part in society's conditioning of the rapist.

What makes a rapist rape? Hatred of women. Low self-esteem. A good opportunity. Alcohol. "Intellectual" rationalizations. Psychosis. Group pressure. The idea of male supremacy. The belief that females are exploitable property. Pornography.

Whether rapists are 'sick" depends on a person's definition of sickness. Suffice it to say that most rapists appear "normal" and do not fit the popular myths of a "loony."

Understanding these rapists' motivations may be the key to your survival.

CHAPTER 6

Passive Resistance, or Fighting with Your Brain

To resist or not to resist?

The answer often elicits confusion. That's because resisting has different connotations to different people. Either of two things may be meant by the advice to fight back. Resistance can mean physical struggling, screaming, or the use of weapons, or it can mean using your mind to stall or trick the rapist.

In 1966, the President's Commission on Law Enforcement and Administration of Justice surveyed 10,000 households to study victimization. Households were asked if anyone in the family had ever been the victim of a rape or rape attempt. Of all the attacks reported, only one-fourth of the rapes had been completed. Three-fourths of the victims had been able to escape.

This survey shows that resistance is possible and overwhelmingly successful. Studying how various victims satisfactorily resisted presents more of a problem because many victims of attempted rapes do not report the attempt. They breathe a prayer of relief and go on their way, either hoping it will never happen again or completely suppressing the incident in their mind, maybe even doubting it happened at all.

However, through rape seminars, self-defense classes, victim interviews, and police records, a pattern of various defense techniques does emerge. From these investigations, police advise passive resistance. This term refers to thinking, talking, and stalling your attacker until you have a chance for escape. Active resistance (discussed in the following chapter) means physical struggling, screaming, and weapons.

Active resistance can be dangerous, because it may antagonize the attacker and make him more violent. He is immediately confronted with the decision either to let you go or to do whatever necessary to shut you up or make you stop struggling.

A rapist usually has a prepared routine; he uses the same line or physical approach on each victim. His ritual has been well practiced. Many researchers say that in the majority of cases, if a girl resists in any way, the attacker will turn and run. He wants a victim who won't give him any trouble and who will be paralyzed with fear and submit to whatever he tells her to do, go wherever he tells her to go.

Any form of resistance, even passive, may throw the attacker off the track. Just a direct stare into his face will discourage some men. Grabbing you from the rear, counting on the darkness to hide his identity, an attacker may have hoped for a quick encounter. A stare may cause him to worry about being caught and send him running for cover.

If, after your first impulsive struggle, you see that the

rapist refuses to run and you cannot overpower him, change your tactics. Say something like, "Okay, you win." Or, "All right, I give up." When you stop struggling and calm him down, you gain time to think about a later escape. Remember, you can always struggle again later when nothing else works.

Your response when attacked is usually fear; let that work for you. If possible, pretend to faint. Some rapists may not want a limp mass in their arms and will run away immediately. Another rapist may think he has hurt you when he grabbed you and run away for fear of being caught guilty of a worse crime.

No matter how the rapist reacts, fainting or appearing to be in a frightened daze gives you time to think. During this stall time, you analyze the situation: How desperate is he for me to submit? What does his expression say? Anger? Fear? Sexual arousal? Poor self-esttem? Is he armed? Where are we? What can I use to escape?

The purpose of the stall is to catch the attacker off guard and to put him in a relaxed mood so you can escape.

Remember that escape outdoors is much easier than indoors. First, try to talk the man into moving you to an outdoor spot where you might see other people who could help you or where you might gain access to a car. Sociologist Pauline Bart found that victims have very often been successful in talking the rapist into letting them choose the place.

One victim pretended to go along but insisted she had to have a cigarette to calm her down. She asked if he could take her to a grocery store to buy a pack. He agreed and stopped at a convenience store, where he went in, leaving her in the car. He promised he'd keep an eye on her, but she made her escape anyway when another car pulled into the parking space beside her.

Another victim pretended to go along but warned that her apartment walls were thin; if there was any noise at all, the next door neighbor would come over to see about her. She suggested they go to a nearby park. He agreed and started to walk her over to the park. As a lighted car pulled into a parking lot nearby, she broke and ran for the car. The driver pulled her inside and took her to report the attack.

If you're caught at home alone, claim that your father or a friend is on his way over and will be arriving any minute. Suggest that you walk somewhere else. If you are obviously frightened about the attack, you can let the information "slip" and hope the rapist will take the initiative to move the attack. Again, in getting him to move the attack to another place, you are buying time. You are increasing your chances of escape by getting outdoors and into the path of others who might come to your rescue. (If your friend or father is *really* on his way over, just stall until the help arrives.)

Ways to stall are only limited by your imagination. Explain that your mother gets worried when you're late and ask if he can drive you to a phone booth to say you'll be late. Or explain that you'll go along with him but could he please drive you somewhere to get birth control protection.

Stalling in a rape attempt is not as difficult as it may seem. Rapists often prolong attacks over several hours because their motivations are not simply sexual. If they are motivated by anger and hatred, they may want to prolong their feeling of power and domination over you and prolong your humiliation and pain. They enjoy seeing your fear and helplessness. They need gloating time.

If a rapist attacks to bolster his sagging self-esteem, he may prolong the rape either to try to win your affection or to get your attention and affirmation that he is important and somebody worth knowing. He may use the prolonged time together to win your sympathy so you won't report him. Or he may want to prolong the attack and, in his mind, turn it into a real "love affair."

Whatever verbal response you use to stall must be based on how you read the rapist's motives. Some experts advise that you be very humble. Others advise that you be assertive and never plead for sympathy. Both responses can be correct with different rapists (as will be discussed later in the chapter). The longer you are with the man—the longer you stall—the better your chances of reading him correctly. Although none of the stalls may work, you've lost nothing by trying.

The following are some passive resistance techniques that have worked:

VERBAL ATTACKS

These are most effective when given immediately upon attack. "Leave me alone." "Get away from here." "I'll call the police." "My boyfriend will be here any minute." "Those people inside can hear you."

These may convince the attacker that you're not a helpless victim and that he will be in for a struggle. Statements like these will be most effective with a rapist who has low self-esteem and doesn't feel too much up to the attack anyway. Also, the opportunity rapist who acted impulsively may just as impulsively run away.

POOR-ME RESPONSES

You may claim to be as depressed and rejected as the rapist is. Say that your mother has cancer and is dying, or that you just flunked out of school, or that your parents just kicked you out of the house, or that you have absolutely no friends and don't care if you die or not. Explain that you're a virgin and say you'll probably kill yourself if he carries out the rape.

A poor-me response is particularly effective with the rapist who attacks because of a low self-image. If he feels rejection and depression like the kind you claim to have, he may identify with you and sympathize. Or if he sees his victims merely as objects for his sexual pleasure, he may begin to see you as a person—a sister or a best friend.

"If a woman can talk and make the rapist see her as a person," Officer H. C. Meell, of the Houston Police Department, says, "there is an excellent chance he will let her go.

This poor-me response is least effective with someone who is raping out of hatred, because the response increases his feeling of power and revenge. He may be raping you because you remind him of a hated wife, ex-girlfriend, or mother. Study his facial expression; does it say hate or depression?

EGO-BUILDER RESPONSE

If you think that your attacker is low man on society's totem pole, try to appear very humble. Avoid any signs of rejection, because he is already acting out of a deep sense of rejection. Mention that he seems like a nice man, and you can't understand why he would be raping someone. Say he is good-looking and probably could date any number of girls if he just went about it in the right way. Explain that you are not rejecting him but that you don't have sex with anyone.

Show him that you know he is strong and powerful, so he won't have to prove it to you.

Appeal to his sense of protection. Say that you are glad he came along, because you are afraid to be out alone at night with so many perverts on the streets. Act as if you assume he only wants to talk to you and that this is just a "social" occasion, that actual rape is far from his mind because he isn't "that kind" of criminal.

MORAL RESPONSES

Unless the rapist is psychotic or completely amoral (without a sense of right and wrong), he might respond to appeals like "God loves you," "God will punish you for this," "You are not that kind of person, are you?" Psychologists insist that even criminals have a moral code and look down on the rapist as being the lowest of the low.

If the rapist is acting out a hostility for women in general, however, this appeal may further anger him by reminding him of some significant, dominating woman in his life.

BODY-WEAKNESS RESPONSE

Tell the attacker that you have cancer; many people believe that cancer is contagious (it isn't). Tell him that you had rheumatic fever as a child and have a bad heart murmur and that you might go into shock from fear. Claim that you are pregnant and that intercourse will cause you to miscarry or may kill you. Warn him that you have a venereal disease.

Some victims have even successfully *acted out* a body weakness—pretended insanity or mental retardation by reciting nursery rhymes, babbling incoherently, laughing uncontrollably. Sign as if you're a deaf mute. Even some rapists have moral codes about helpless victims. (There are exceptions, such as the male nurse who repeatedly raped a paralyzed patient who could only signal what was happening to her by lifting one finger.)

Body weakness claims are most effective on the opportunist rapist, the drunk rapist, and the sexually motivated rapist. Such attackers rarely intend to permanently hurt their victims, if for no other reason than that conviction is more likely and the penalty stiffer.

GROUP RESPONSE

Verbal responses to a group attack, of course, may overlap the other suggested appeals, but dealing with a group presents special difficulties. First, find the leader of the group. He will usually be the one who is doing all the talking, encouraging the others, setting up the scene. He'll usually be the first one who attempts to rape you. Generally, the others will be watching him, to make sure that he approves of their words and actions.

Second, when you think you have spotted the leader or

the boldest of the group, try to get him alone. Pretend to go along with the rape but say it will be better if you go off somewhere together. Get him to drive you some place completely private. Promise to come back to the others later. However, don't put down the others. If insulted, they may take matters into their own hands. The stall and change of scene give you more time to think and escape.

If you have a girlfriend with you when attacked, get her to pretend too. Make out like you are on their side, and you don't understand why she won't go along.

Once you have divided one attacker from the rest, you have a better chance of escape. Try one of the other verbal appeals already mentioned. Perhaps just getting the leader or other group member away from the peer pressure will give him an out from the rape. He may have been "participating" or "going along" only halfheartedly, afraid of what the others would think.

Whichever verbal response you use to stall and discourage your attacker, make sure you are a good actor. Put your heart into the act; you must be convincing.

Besides verbal attempts to resist, victims have been successful in stopping an attack by doing crude, unfeminine things. If you feel sick (as many victims do when forced into sexual acts), don't turn away to vomit; throw up on the offender. Or, force yourself to vomit by turning your head away and sticking your finger down your throat.

If you have to go to the bathroom, don't ask to go somewhere else (unless there's a restroom nearby which might give you a way to escape). Urinate on the rapist or your own clothes. Both vomiting and urinating are offensive to the attacker and will sometimes make him leave you alone. Belching and scratching are also turn-offs which have deterred rapists from finishing an attack.

If, despite the stall, the verbal appeals, and the crudeness, the rapist is persistent, police advise that you submit, especially if he is armed.

Even during submission, there are still things you can do to protect yourself from further psychological harm. Talk to the man and keep reminding him that you are a person. Say things like, "I can't breathe," or "You're too heavy." Make him keep in the forefront of his mind that he is dealing with a real, live person—not an inanimate object.

Don't struggle during the actual rape. Often a struggle further excites the person, makes him think you are enjoying the rape, or makes him use more force or violence.

Try to disengage your mind from the attack. Concentrate on memorizing his face, hair, eye color, any scars, and so on. Remember and rehash over and over in your mind what he has said to you, his tone of voice, whether he has a stutter or a lisp or uses a strange dialect. This will help your recall when you report the incident to the police. Because rapists often say the same things to all their victims, police can sometimes put together a pattern to catch the man.

Never give the rapist your correct last name. Make up a name. That way he can never trace you and find out where you live.

After the attack, assure the man that you want nothing but secrecy, that you will not report the attack, and that you fear him. Most rapists feel relatively sure they will never be caught, and consequently, they leave victims without doing them further harm. Perhaps they rely on the old taboo in society that rape is something for the victim to be ashamed of, that she will never tell. Whatever your attacker's reason for feeling you are not much threat, go along. Otherwise, he may think he has to kill you to keep from being identified.

Passive resistance—trying to talk, think, and stall your way out of the attack—allows you to bide your time until the scene changes, until the rapist changes his mind, or until someone comes to your rescue. All are very real possibilities.

CHAPTER 7

Active Resistance, or Fighting with Your Muscle

Blood-curdling screams and uppercuts to the chin are about as foreign to most girls' repertoire as bull-fighting. Although girls receive much more training in athletics and physical fitness than they used to, many girls still believe that too much activity will build unsightly muscles, that boys don't like loudmouths, that a girl shouldn't beat her boyfriend at tennis, that wearing high heels to make their legs look curvy is more important than mobility and comfort, that they should dial the phone with a pencil to prevent breaking their long nails.

With all that "weak-is-beautiful" conditioning, it's no wonder that 50 percent of rape victims (Amir's study) refuse to resist an attacker in any way. In 87 percent of the cases studied, only verbal threats were initially used to get the victim to submit.

Victims are startled and paralyzed by fear when a rapist grabs them and orders them to come along or drive somewhere. Although such fear is perfectly understandable (who hasn't heard of victims who've been brutally murdered?), a victim's best defense is to try to overcome that initial fear and use her mind, and muscle if necessary, to escape.

If she can resist in any way, studies indicate that the majority of attackers let the victim go.

How do you overcome that initial paralyzing fear?

First, an alert attitude helps. Be aware of potentially dangerous places and circumstances. Realize that rape can happen to you. Prepare for it by considering how you might react if attacked. Second, educate yourself to the way rapists work. Third, be alert to their motivations and what may appease or anger them. Finally, realize that you have a good defense in a clear mind and an able body.

In the last chapter we talked about fighting with your mind (passive resistance) and about the equal advantage you have with a rapist who has a practiced routine and takes your submission for granted. When you resist, you throw a kink in his routine; he has to react with an unwritten script, as you do.

But an able body? you ask. Yes, you've at least got the raw materials of an able body. Think back to when you were younger. If you have a brother or sister, can't you remember a few arguments when you landed some painful wallops? How about in second grade when you outran all the boys in a footrace. How about the time you fell out of a tree in the backyard and screamed your lungs out until a neighbor heard you and came running?

Naturally, you've passed the catching up time between boys and girls. Doctors tell us most girls are bigger and stronger than boys in the early years of life. Then, just before and during puberty, boys catch up and surpass girls in size. But size is not the whole story. Strength, coordination, skill, training, conditioning, and cunning enter the picture when determining your ability to fight.

In the last decade, some girls have begun to shed the weak-is-beautiful syndrome. They have insisted on joining Little League sports. School programs as well as families have linked up with the national jogging fervor. Colleges have channeled more money into women's sports. Enrollment in self-defense courses has grown. Girls are no longer bragging of a weak, out-of-condition body. In fact, some are even flaunting the opposite—reports of abusive wives and battered husbands have become a popular topic.

This changing attitude is reflected in rape studies. Carolyn Hursch, in her study on rape, found that girls in their teens are much more likely to resist an attacker physically than older females. Their confidence to resist probably comes from the fact that they are more active than older women and feel more fit.

Although most police and rape crisis workers advise passive resistance, others advise differently. Susan Brownmiller, who's done extensive interpretation of rape studies, concludes that even complete submission gives no blanket assurance that a victim won't be hurt. More recently, two 1980 studies done by the National Center for the Prevention and Control of Rape show that women who resist an attack are more likely to escape and run no greater risk of injury than those who submit. *No* study has ever shown that resistance provokes a rapist to murder.

Should you or shouldn't you struggle?

First, determine whether the attacker has a weapon. Amir's Philadelphia study found that only 20 percent of the rapists carried a weapon. A New York study found that only one-third were armed. In almost all cases, however, the knife or gun was used only to frighten the victim into submission rather than to brutalize or murder.

Generally, when a rapist has a weapon, he lets you know immediately, as in the following cases:

> There were two in the car and they stopped to ask if I wanted a ride, to which I said no. The passenger jumped out and grabbed my arm and started pulling me toward the car. When I wouldn't go, he pulled a knife out and put it to my throat and told me to get in. I did.

Another victim says:

> I was letting my car warm up a minute before starting to the store. I looked up and saw a man walking in front of my car, but I thought he was going to pass by. Then he came between my car and the next one to me, and he tried to open the door, but it was locked. When he couldn't get the door open, he pulled a revolver-type gun from his pants and held it right at the window and told me to open the door. I opened the door; I was scared to death!

Both of these victims did exactly the right thing. *Never* resist when the attacker is armed. Do not run or scream. If you resist, he may have to use the weapon to prove that he means business. In the cases above (as in the vast majority of attacks), the attacker did not use the weapon on the victim; he only ensured her cooperation.

If you've determined that he's unarmed and has no friend with him, the second consideration is his size. If you think you are almost equal in size and as skilled, coordinated, and determined as your attacker, fight.

And do so immediately. Law officers all agree on that one point: If you are going to fight, do it at the instant the man attacks. You have the advantage of catching him off guard because he's expecting you to submit without a struggle. If you resist immediately, he can quickly change his mind and look for an easier victim. If you wait until later, he may get angry.

The decision to struggle involves lots of "ifs" on split-second notice. But then that's the purpose of this book: to give you advance notice and help you think through the whys and hows of rape attacks and plan possible responses.

If you determine that the attacker has no weapon, that he is alone, and that you are going to resist, remember that the aim of the fight is not to knock him out; you are merely struggling to escape, for a chance to pull away, run, and attract someone's attention.

SCREAMING

Screams are the easiest defense. They do not come naturally to most girls. Shrieks, yes. Irritated little cries, yes. Surprised screams of delight, yes. But loud, blood-curdling screams, no.

When you're out driving with all the windows up, practice a few screams. You might surprise yourself with how much sound you can muster. Screams have to be loud to be heard over a stereo playing next door, or the motor, air-conditioner, and radio in someone's car. If you let out a dynamic scream, the attacker may fear that you'll bring the whole apartment building to your rescue, and he may flee before it's too late.

But screams are not always the key to getting away. They may be mistaken for a distressed heroine on a television drama next door. Or they may be ignored, no matter how loud and urgent they seem. Remember never to scream "help." If someone recognizes your scream as trouble, he may fear getting involved. Or, he may ignore it thinking you're involved in a family or lover's quarrel.

Yelling "fire" is your best bet. For selfish reasons, people respond to that scream. Finally, remember that screams make the rapist nervous. When you're out in a deserted area where no one can hear you and come to your rescue anyway, save your energy.

WEAPONS

You can buy various chemical sprays inexpensively at most hardware or discount stores. They can temporarily blind the attacker, long enough for you to escape. You can also make your own spray of lemon juice or red pepper in a plastic squeeze lemon. Breath spray, hair spray, and perfume can also blind someone.

There are a couple of problems with these sprays, however. One is getting your hands on them in a second's notice. Most girls carry them in the bottom of their purse. That's no good. You'll seldom have time to fish them out for use, and chances are that your purse will be knocked from your hands. The second disadvantage with sprays is that they must be used at close range and with the wind's direction to be effective. If you carry a spray with you, have it in your hand as you start across campus or approach any area where you think you might need it.

Other weapons you might have with you include a corkscrew, metal nail file, keys draped through your knuckles, belt buckle, jewelry, books, umbrella. These weapons don't sound as though they could incapacitate anyone, but remember, you only need a moment to escape.

With any of these weapons, particularly the umbrella, don't swing. Jab. The rapist can catch or knock away a swing, which isn't all that powerful anyway. Jab at his unprotected areas like the eyes, the upper lip, the bridge of the nose.

Remember that any of these weapons can be taken away and used against you. If you decide to use a weapon, have it handy, aim at a sensitive spot, and run when you get loose.

HOLDS, BLOWS, KICKS, BITES

Maybe all that's necessary for you to escape is to break the rapist's hold and run to safety. If an attacker grabs you from behind, bob your head back forcefully against his face and nose. This is particularly effective if he is against a wall or other hard surface. The back of your head is much harder than the thin tissues across the bridge of his nose. Then stomp down hard on his instep.

If the attacker grabs your arm or wrist, jerk quickly in the direction of his thumb. The thumb is the weakest part of the grip. Pull it away from the rest of his hand. If he grabs your wrists, push both your arms outward and up. He will automatically counter by trying to force them back in.

When he does, quickly jerk your arms together and up over your head.

If he is choking you, turn your face into the crook of his elbow. This will take the pressure off the front of your throat and allow you to breathe.

Talk to him, trying to break his concentration. Surprise him by jerks and blows while you're talking.

Bite him in the fleshy part of his hand between the thumb and forefinger, or bite the back of his hand where the blood vessels are. Poke your fingers in his eyes. Scratch his face. Yank off his glasses. Spit in his eyes. Pull his hair. Twist his ears. Use the side of your open hand for strikes. Aim at his kidneys, nose, upper lip, throat, or under his chin.

Use thrust kicks. Bring your knee up parallel to the floor and then swing your lower leg straight out with a snap. Aim your kicks at the attacker's kneecap. Aiming too high will cause you to lose your balance, or he may grab your foot and throw you down.

The man may demand that you lie down. This can work to your favor: his larger size will be less of an advantage when he is off his feet. If you are quick and can out-maneuver him, you may get away easier from a lying position. His lying down has one other major advantage for you. You can get close enough to him to really incapacitate him. Storaska and Bennett recommend three ways to completely defeat your attacker. All three of these attacks depend on your pretending to go along with the rapist. If you have struggled earlier, pretend that you have given up and that you no longer intend to fight. Try to gain his confidence that you are subdued. If you have not struggled previously, pretend that you are a willing participant in the rape.

Place your hands on the sides of the rapist's face, gently caressing him and pulling him forward as if you were going to kiss him. (Numerous cases suggest that many rapists think the victim enjoys the rape and plead with her to pretend that the attack is a love encounter.) Gradually put both thumbs over his eyes and press very hard. You are pressing your hands into his eyesockets. If you press hard enough, he will go into shock.

A second defense is to place your hands on the sides of the rapist's head as if pulling him forward for a kiss. Then press very hard just below the earlobes where the jaw and skull meet, the spot of numerous nerve endings. You have to press exactly the correct spot, so ask your family doctor sometime to show you where this nerve center is located.

A third defense is to caress him; and when he is unsuspecting, grab and squeeze his testicles. This will throw him into shock or at least disable him long enough for you to escape. Males are very protective of the groin area and will not let you get close enough for such an attack unless they are convinced you are willing, submissive, or too frightened to put up a fight.

Only you can decide in any given situation if and how to struggle when attacked. Most women must psychologically prepare themselves *beforehand, in a general way*, to use injuring force or even a weapon. If the rapist has a weapon or becomes violent, go along with his requests. Resisting rape is not worth your life.

PART THREE

After an Attack— What to Do

CHAPTER 8

Get Medical Help

Kathi, sixteen, left the house after another heated argument with her parents about the car. After persuading them one more time that she wouldn't be out late and that she'd take a friend along, she attended a junior varsity football game.

After dropping off her girlfriend on the way home, she stopped by a convenience store for a copy of *Seventeen*. The only other customer in the store followed her out. Once outside, he pulled a knife and told her to get in her car and drive them to the nearby park. After he raped her and ran off into the darkness, she pulled her clothes back on and sat in the car dumbfounded.

She knew she couldn't recognize him. During the attack he had ordered her to turn away and shoved at her face when she tried to look at him. Crying and clutching the steering wheel, she tried to pull herself together and decide what to do.

If she told her parents, they would never let her have the car again. They would blame her for stopping without permission and would probably keep her under lock and key every night. She just couldn't tell them. If she couldn't identify the attacker, what good would telling anybody do?

She finally drove home and went straight to her room under the pretext of reading the magazine. The full impact of what had happened didn't hit her until the next day, when she told her girlfriend. What if she got VD or became pregnant? Her friend knew her parents and was equally concerned about their reaction but encouraged her to tell them anyway. Kathi hesitated another two days. She felt calmer and less afraid; she felt she could put the incident behind her if she really tried.

She never told her parents.

Kathi was one of the luckier victims. She was not seriously injured, she didn't develop VD, and she didn't get pregnant. Other victims do not fare so well.

Injuries and other aftereffects of rape include weak pulse, paleness, chills, slurred or slowed speech, loss of appetite, uncontrollable crying, insomnia, over-all muscle soreness, vaginal infections, cuts, bruises, broken bones, bladder and anus injury, cigarette burns, and even death.

Even if you experience none of the more serious physical injuries from rape, you should still get a medical exam. If you and your parents later decide to press charges, you'll have no case without medical evidence. If you develop venereal disease or get pregnant, you'll need even further medical treatment.

Time is very important. The longer you wait to report to the doctor or hospital for an exam, the less likely there will be evidence of the rape. However, there is no set procedure about whether you should report to the hospital or the police first. If you call the police, they will make a brief report. Then, if you have no other transportation, they will drive you to the hospital for the medical exam.

If you go to the hospital first, be sure to choose a hospital that handles rape victims and follows the correct exam procedures. Some private hospitals don't handle rape victims. Others don't want any legal involvement. Although you might be more comfortable in choosing a family doctor, he and his staff may not be trained to follow the correct procedures in the exam so as to preserve the evidence for police records. Most large city hospitals have staff and doctors who are specially trained to recognize rape injuries, to understand your emotional upset, and to gather evidence for a strong case. Such hospitals are the best choice. At the time of the attack, most victims are too confused to think clearly about a hospital, police reporting, where to go, whom to tell. Find out now—before a crisis—which hospitals in your city handle rape victims.

As soon after the attack as possible, tell anyone who happens to be nearby—a clerk in a store, a driver in a passing car, someone at home in a nearby lighted house. These people will bear witness (in court, if necessary) that you told them about the attack immediately and that you appeared to be upset. Then phone your parents or a friend to go with you for the medical exam. If neither is available, phone the rape crisis center listed in the yellow or white pages of the phone book. Most centers provide escort service to the hospital. If you are underage, however, your parents will need to sign before you can be treated.

On the way to the hospital, tell your parent or friend all the details of the attack while you can still remember them. They can help you to recall all the details later when you report the rape to the police. (Remembering every detail is extremely important, as I'll mention in the next chapter.)

Payment should not be a matter of concern. Payment for the medical exam is sometimes covered by your parent's accidental insurance policy. In some states, there are special agencies, private groups, and organizations which pay for the treatment of victims. Sometimes the police or district attorney's office pays for the exam.

If you report to an emergency room staffed with trained doctors and nurses, you will be given the best of care. Recognizing your emotional upset, they will probably lead you to a private room to wait for the gynecologist (a doctor trained to treat female diseases and problems). While you are at the hospital, you may also be counseled by a psychologist, who will help you and your family deal with the emotional and psychological trauma of the rape.

Someone will also give you information about any follow-up treatment necessary—where, when, and how to get it. You will also be told how to report the rape to the police, if you haven't already done so. If you decide to press charges later and your case goes to court, the doctor or counselor may be called as a witness about the attack and your emotional and physical condition.

If you report to a smaller or less efficient hospital emergency room, your medical exam may not go as quickly. Since your injury is internal and emotional as well as physical, your emergency may seem less critical than that of someone who's bleeding profusely. Rather than becoming more upset, try to understand that the delay or brusque treatment is due to a lack of training and ignorance about your condition rather than a personal affront.

During the medical exam, the doctor or nurse will take

your medical history and ask you questions about your physical condition before the rape so that he or she can make a thorough exam. The questions are personal and might be embarrassing to you. Are you a virgin? Have you ever used birth control? What type? When was your last menstrual period? Have you ever had any vaginal itching or infections? Was the man who attacked you using a condom? Have you had a bath or douche since the attack? Remember that the questions are necessary for the doctor to know what to look for during the exam and what follow-up treatment to advise. After completing the medical history form, the doctor will begin the physical exam and take evidence that you may want to use later in a court trial.

The doctor will ask you to lie down on the examining table, and the nurse will drape a sheet over you. He will insert an instrument called a speculum into your vagina to check for sperm from the attacker and for any other signs of intercourse such as a torn hymen. The blood type of a rapist can be identified from his seminal fluid. He will rub a long cotton swab against the lining of the vagina and place the smear on a slide for microscopic examination. The doctor will also note any cuts, tears, bruises, or redness around the rectum and genital area. This part of the exam will probably take less than five minutes.

After the pelvic exam, the doctor will examine the rest of your body for any kind of foreign matter such as skin and hairs from the attacker. He will take a scraping from under your fingernails, where such things often collect if you have struggled with the rapist. He will also take samples of your own hair to compare with foreign hairs from the attacker. Finally, he will check your clothes for the same evidence of the rape—hairs, blood, semen, and other stains. If there are blood stains, he will take samples to type the attacker's blood.

Finally, the doctor will check other parts of your body for teethmarks, bruises, cuts, or redness. Red marks that result from the attacker's holding you down, hitting you, or squeezing you go away after a few hours. This is another reason you need to get medical attention as soon as possible after the attack.

If the doctor misses any marks or bruises, be sure to point them out to him so he can examine and record them.

Either the doctor or the nurse may take photographs of your injuries to be used later in court if you decide to press charges.

All this evidence will be taken very carefully, labeled, and sealed according to legal procedures. Some police departments provide hospitals with special forms, containers, slides, and labels to be used in the collection process. Evidence has to be sealed, correctly labeled, and passed through the correct chain of custody. If there's a mistake somewhere along the line and something is not labeled correctly or sealed, the evidence may not be admissible in court.

The evidence will be kept for a certain period of time. If you decide to press charges during this time, the evidence will be turned over to the police. If you have already decided to press charges, the evidence will be sent to the police immediately. After collecting the evidence, the doctor will treat any injuries you have.

Finally, he will advise you and your parents about treatment for possible pregnancy. The danger for pregnancy is higher when you have been raped ten to eighteen days before the start of your menstrual cycle, your fertile period. If your period has just ended or is just about to begin, the doctor may not advise that you take treatment to avoid pregnancy. Rather, he may suggest that you wait and see if pregnancy develops. Then, if your period is more than two weeks late, he will give you a pregnancy test. If that test is positive, you may have a medical extraction, which aborts an early pregnancy.

If the rape attack is during your fertile period, the doctor will probably advise DES, commonly called "morning after" pills. The DES pills or injections cause a hormone imbalance and may make you sick. You may be nauseated, lose your appetite, or have diarrhea, dizziness, headaches, cramps, or swelling in your breasts. Again, because DES is only effective if taken within twenty-four hours after the rape, you need medical help as soon as possible.

Tests for venereal disease may also be given at a later visit. Symptoms of gonorrhea may appear from one to two weeks after rape, and symptoms of syphilis may appear four to six weeks after rape. Taking the VD tests at the time of the attack will only verify that you didn't have the diseases before. If a venereal disease is diagnosed at this follow-up exam, you will be treated at that time.

If during the medical exam, the doctor seems abrupt or nontalkative, he may be having his own emotional reaction. Some doctors may appear unfeeling, or at least unaware of how emotionally upset you are, because they are untrained in handling the rape victim's trauma. Other doctors may be very formal and impersonal because they are concentrating on following the procedures correctly and being careful with all the evidence.

The doctor or nurse may even be angry about the attack.

A doctor who sees very emotionally upset or seriously injured victims often feels angry at the attackers who brutalize women. The doctor may feel helpless to ease your discomfort because there is really little he or she can do after the attack. Don't mistake a doctor's or nurse's stern expression for anger at you, but rather interpret it as dismay at the situation and the attacker.

If you have never had a pelvic exam before, the procedures I've described may seem strange and frightening. The pelvic exam done by a competent doctor is not painful, unless you have extensive injuries. Feel free to ask questions about any of the procedures or treatment you don't understand.

Knowing beforehand what to expect should make the experience easier if you ever find yourself in such a crisis. Fearing the unknown is usually much worse than the procedure or event itself.

Regardless of what you decide about reporting to the police, get medical help immediately. You owe it to yourself for your physical well-being and peace of mind.

CHAPTER **9**

Get Legal Help

The time to decide to report rape is now—before there's any pressure from parents or friends, before there's any threat from a rapist, before you're confused and dulled by shock. The only way to clear the streets of rapists and to unbottle the anger inside you is to cooperate with police by reporting.

Reporting rape does not necessarily mean pressing charges and going to court. Even if you do not file charges, your report helps police put together the rapist's pattern of attack. They note patterns in places where he attacks, the disguises and "lines" he uses, and what he says and does during the attack. Linking such details from several cases often helps the police catch the offender.

Admittedly, there are reasons for not reporting rape. Fear is one. Perhaps the rapist has threatened to find you later or to hurt your little brother. However, unless the rapist stole your wallet or got your address some other way, he is not likely to be able to carry out such a threat. (Lieutenant E. P. Morrow, who has had almost ten years experience dealing with rape in the Houston area, says that he knows of only one case where the attacker was successful in carrying out his threat.) Many victims, though, move or change phone numbers or schedules to feel safer.

Other victims fail to report because they think that even if the rapist is caught, nothing will be done. While it is true that conviction rates are low, something can often be done. Even if the rapist is not located immediately, the police become familiar with his tactics and have a better chance of catching him on the next attack. Just because conviction rates are low, there's no point in adding to the problem. Failing to report certainly doesn't change the picture or cut down on the crime.

Some victims don't report the attack because their parents discourage them. These parents don't want to prosecute because they want to spare their daughters the trauma of the trial. If your parents feel like this, remind them that reporting is not the same as prosecuting. If you do want to prosecute and get the rapist off the streets, you may have to encourage your parents to go along with your decision.

Another reason victims fail to report is that they know the rapist. They fear hurting everyone involved, especially if the rapist or his family is close to theirs. One officer remarks, "About 60 percent of all murders are committed by acquaintances, too, but that doesn't stop murder charges from being filed."

Only you can decide if you want to keep your social connection to the rapist intact to the extent that you will remain quiet about such a psychological injury. If you do decide that you cannot bring charges against the acquaintance, report the incident anyway. The police can put enough pressure on him that he will certainly not repeat the attack. They can pick him up, question him, and warn him that he has been reported and is being watched. This pressure will go a long way toward keeping him clear of you in the future.

Finally, a victim may hesitate to report the rape because the rapist has tried to turn the attack into a social call. He may apologize, explain that his family would be hurt, and beg you to feel sorry for him and not report it. If you are sympathetic, he has gotten away with raping you and is free to attack someone else in the future.

All these factors together explain why, nationally, nine out of ten victims never report a rape. The picture is not so grim in cities and states where women's groups, police, and other law agencies have encouraged reporting. Lieutenant Morrow, of the Harris County Sheriff's Department, estimates that one in four rapes is now being reported in the Houston area.

To encourage even more reporting, police have even gone so far as to allow third-party reports. They will take information about a rape from an anonymous victim, from a family member, or from a rape crisis center volunteer working with the victim.

When a victim reports, she allows her emotional wounds to heal in retelling the crime and in doing something constructive about the attack. She provides information that may solve other rape cases, and she starts the chain of events if she decides to prosecute later. Delay in reporting adds to the rapist's chances for escape and dulls your memory. Delay also weakens your case if you later press charges. Decide now that you will report a rape—for your own good and that of other potential victims.

Reporting rape can be done either before or after the

medical exam. If you have the medical exam first, the hospital will give you the sealed evidence to turn over to the police.

Generally, police follow this procedure for the reporting:

1. When you call, they send a policeman to the scene of the crime and question you briefly about the attack.
2. If you are badly injured, they drive you to the hospital. If possible, your parent or a friend can drive you to the hospital.
3. You go to police headquarters to give a more detailed statement. You work with the police artist to compose a picture of the attacker.

If you do not want to press charges, the reporting ends here. If you go to the hospital before calling the police, reporting only involves step 3 above.

If you want to press charges, you continue the reporting process:

4. You go home and wait and cooperate with the police in locating a suspect.
5. When a suspect is arrested, you will be asked to make an identification. There will be a preliminary hearing to see if there's sufficient evidence for a trial. If not, the case will be dropped. If there is enough evidence, the suspect will be charged and the trial date set.
6. You will testify as a primary witness in the trial.

This process from reporting the rape to the end of the trial may last from several months to several years.

Let's go back now through these reporting and prosecuting steps in detail. Knowing what each step involves will help you make a more intelligent decision about reporting and/or filing charges.

STEP 1: THE INITIAL STATEMENT WITH POLICE

When you call the police, usually the nearest policeman will come to the scene or to your home. This policeman will take a brief statement from you about what happened. He will want a description of the attacker and will immediately put out a bulletin on him so that he may be caught if he is still in the area.

Next, the officer will investigate the scene and check for objects that might have fingerprints. It's important for you to leave everything just as it was after the attack—overturned furniture, unlocked windows, and so forth. The police will take pictures to be used as evidence later if you press charges.

Next, the officer will try to find witnesses of the attack. Anyone who heard you scream or saw you after the attack will be questioned. If you do not want your neighbors to know about the report, police can merely say that a crime was committed. In rape cases, officers try to be discreet in their investigation.

Before this initial visit, do not destroy any evidence. That means don't change clothes, don't move anything, don't take a bath, don't wash your face or hands, don't comb your hair, don't even try to calm yourself. Visual evidence of the attack is an important part of the first report. The police will note everything about your appearance and composure, which will be circumstantial evidence that you have been attacked.

STEP 2: MEDICAL EXAM (discussed in last chapter)

Police will drive you to the hospital if you have not already had a medical exam. But because of staff shortages, they will first suggest that a friend or parent drive you. After the exam you will carry the sealed evidence from the exam to the police headquarters.

STEP 3: FORMAL QUESTIONING AND WRITTEN STATEMENT

Many police departments now have specialized rape squads. These people are trained to understand your particular emotional upset and to meet your specific needs. Women officers are usually on the rape squad because police have found that a victim is more at ease in discussing the rape with another woman. If the police department does not have a special rape squad, you may talk to any woman officer there, if you prefer to. Whether you talk with a male or female officer, though, their training and understanding is much more important than their sex.

When the questioning begins, you will be interviewed away from anyone who came with you. Victims feel much freer to describe the details of the attack without someone they know listening. During the interview, you may feel talkative or quiet, be very upset or calm, may cry or remain dry-eyed. All victims react differently; don't worry about your composure.

When the police officer begins the interview, she may use a standardized questionnaire or ask her own questions in her own order. If she uses a standardized form, don't think that she's treating you like a computer number. Generally, an officer uses a form questionnaire to make sure she doesn't miss any detail that will be needed for evidence or whose lack could jeopardize the case later. This questionnaire is an aid in conducting the interview correctly.

An officer may ask questions in her own order because she feels that doing so makes you more relaxed. She can read your mood and ask questions that you seem ready to answer. If you are very upset, she can dwell on mechanical details, such as the color of the rapist's hair. When you are more composed, she can ask for other details such as exactly what the rapist said or did to you.

You'll find that police often ask the same questions over and over again. The purpose is to get you to remember additional details with each retelling. You know yourself that each time you tell a friend about an incident, you leave out or include different details. It is the same with rape accounts.

Do not leave out *any* details of the attack or details leading up to it. Even if you think a particular detail might be damaging to your case, tell the officer anyway. If the rapist tells his attorney and they find this detail missing in your statement, they will point out this discrepancy and try to make it look as though you were lying about the whole incident.

If you don't understand a term the officer uses or a question she asks, she will explain it to you. If you intend to press charges, the police may ask that you leave your clothes (if you brought a change of clothes with you) or ask that you bring them back later for evidence.

After all the information has been assembled, a clerk will

type your statement about the attack and ask you to sign it.
The police will immediately feed this information about the
attack and the attacker into their computer or other system
of information in an effort to develop a picture of the rapist's "modus operandi," (mode of operation)—words,
places, disguises the rapist uses in each attack.

After the interview and statement, you will be asked to
help develop a visual picture of the attacker. A police composite artist will ask you to describe the attacker while he
puts together a picture. Most police departments have
photo kits with hundreds of overlays of different facial parts
—noses, hairlines, eyes, chins. The technician will work
with your description and the overlays until he has a good
likeness of the attacker. Then he will make a copy of the
final product.

Police artist J. D. Satcher concludes that generally the
victim's first impression is the most precise. He prefers to
work with the victim immediately after the attack, while the
rapist's face is still fresh on her mind and before other faces
blend into her consciousness.

Helping compose a picture is often difficult for the victim
because she wants to suppress the incident and forget the
rapist's face. However, with patience, a good technician can
usually come up with a fairly close likeness. In fact, one of
Sergeant Satcher's composites was so accurate the defense
attorney argued that the photo had been made after the
defendant's arrest. The composite, signed and dated
before the arrest, stood up in court.

Occasionally, more creative methods of composing a picture are used. George Powell of the Galveston Police
Department hypnotized, with her permission, a sixteen-
year-old victim who could not remember details of her

attacker's face. Powell was able to get sufficient information from the hypnotized teen to lead to the arrest of her attacker.

After making the formal statement and the composite picture, you go home to wait until something further develops from the clues.

STEP 4: POLICE INVESTIGATION

If you can name your attacker, the police will pick him up immediately for questioning. If you're attacked by a stranger, the police gather clues from your statement and the photo and try to match similarities from other cases. If you were able to get a license number or pinpoint the scene of the attack, they begin tracing the car owner or questioning people who may have been witnesses near the attack scene.

When the police locate a suspect, they will bring him in for processing and for your identification. He will be put in a line-up much like the kind you have probably seen on television. You will be hidden away from the suspect where he can neither see nor hear you.

Identifying the man may be difficult because the rapist often changes his appearance. He may have shaved or, if enough time has passed, grown a beard or mustache. He will be wearing different clothes and may try to adopt a different posture. A person always looks somewhat different standing under bright lights instead of in dark shadows.

You may ask the police officer to have the suspect turn or stand at different angles or speak so that you can try to recognize his voice. If you can make a positive identification, the suspect is arrested and the case is turned over to the district attorney.

Not all police investigations end in the arrest of a suspect. Some lead nowhere, and eventually the cases are marked "unfounded" and dropped. Unfounded means different things in police departments across the country. Often police categorize cases as unfounded for reasons of practicality. If, after reviewing the case, they think conviction is almost impossible, they do not pursue it. For instance, any of the following might fall into the unfounded category in different police departments:

- If the girl waits too long to report the rape or refuses to have a medical exam. (No evidence for the trial.)
- If she's been drinking, taking drugs, or hitchhiking. (Most juries would think she couldn't remember what happened or was "asking for trouble.")
- If she knows the male well or was dating him. (It's his word against hers. The district attorney could not prove without reasonable doubt that she had not agreed to intercourse. But injury, witnesses, or lie detector test results would change the picture.)
- If she is too young or confused or just doesn't want to go through with the trial. (She is the prosecution's only witness and must be able to give her testimony.)
- If she is lying. (About 2 to 3 percent of all cases fall in this category; the girl may have stayed out all night and made up the excuse for her parents. She may need an excuse for being pregnant or having venereal disease. Occasionally, revenge is a motive. Police say these cases fall apart quickly under parental and police interviewing.)

Note that in four of the five categories above, unfounded

does not mean that there is no rape or that the victim is not believed. Rather, unfounded means that the case would be almost impossible to prove in court for one reason or another.

Some police departments give all victims a lie detector test as a matter of routine investigation. Other departments give a lie detector test only when questionable matters surface. Some victims are insulted when they're asked to take the test because they feel it implies they are lying. From the viewpoint of the police, however, the test culls out the few who are lying, and allows them to get on with investigating other cases, saves investigative work, and strengthens other evidence. Taking the test may be in the victim's interest if she falls into one of the other categories, like having been raped on a date. Her passing a lie detector test would strengthen her case and encourage the district attorney to try to prosecute.

Occasionally, a victim may be treated rudely by a police officer. He may seem uninterested in her report or grumpy or angry. He may give the impression that he doesn't care what has just happened to her. Let's look at some of the reasons an officer may act this way.

He or she may be rude, grumpy, and uninterested for the same reasons store clerks, secretaries, or bankers may be— he may not like his job or may have other personal problems. He may have sick children or a boss who's been on his back all morning. He may be rude or uninterested because he is untrained. Although many police departments have psychologists who work with them on rape cases to help them understand a victim's emotional feelings, not all police officers receive this training. Often an emergency rape call is answered by the policeman who happens to be nearest, and he may be the least likely to be trained in this special area. Once at headquarters for formal interviewing, the victim is usually taken care of by more trained, understanding officers.

An officer may act uninterested because he feels that the whole report will be useless. If he arrives at the scene and the girl has bathed or changed clothes, the evidence is destroyed. He will fill out the forms, but he knows that there will be no evidence for a court trial and no chance for conviction.

Sometimes he is unenthusiastic about the investigation because he knows that about one-third of the victims will not follow through and try to help him catch the rapist. Either their parents will refuse to let them go through the trial or the police department itself will decide that it takes too much time and is too upsetting for the victim.

A police officer may be brusque and businesslike because he feels inadequate. He is angry with the whole justice system that makes the conviction of rapists difficult. He may feel helpless to console the victim and unable to promise her that the police can catch the attacker. He may feel embarrassed, especially if you remind him of a young teenager he knows. He may be angry that females put themselves in dangerous situations without adequate precautions. He knows how often law agencies, schools, and other organizations warn victims about hitchhiking or keeping car doors or houses unlocked. Because a policeman is trained to always be on the alert for dangerous traps, he finds it hard to understand why others are not cautious enough about their own safety.

If, for any of these reasons, you have been treated unfairly or rudely, understanding the policeman's viewpoint may improve the situation. Regardless of the reason, you do not have to put up with rude treatment. You can get the police officer's name and badge number, and you or your parents can report him to his supervisor, the chief of police, or the mayor, if necessary. Police departments want to keep the public's goodwill. They will check out your complaints to see that such behavior is stopped.

With the spotlight increasingly on the crime of rape and on police handling of rape victims, the vast majority of police officers dealing with rape have received adequate training to help you and will treat you with respect and courtesy. They want to get the rapists off the streets. That's their job.

The Decision About Going to Court

When a suspect is in custody, the police turn the case over to the prosecutor. He looks at the following material and decides whether he has a strong enough case to go to trial.

- whether the rape events indicate prior planning by the attacker
- prior relationship between victim and attacker
- past sexual history of the victim
- past sexual history of the attacker
- semen or blood on clothing of the accused or victim
- conduct of accused when he was arrested
- opportunity of the accused to commit the assault
- flight of the accused

- presence of a weapon
- confession
- age difference (big gap in age more likely to support evidence of rape)
- victim's appearance (torn clothing, emotional upset)
- medical evidence (semen in the vagina, bruises, cuts, redness)
- drinking and drugs involved
- time lapse before victim reported incident
- witnesses to victim's upset; promptness of complaint to family, friend, other witness
- lack of motive to make false report
- lie detector test results

Because rape is a crime against the state—against public decency and morals—rather than against the individual, the district attorney has the final authority to decide if the case will be tried. But no matter how strong the case may be, you hold the final key; you are the state's chief witness. If you will not testify, the DA cannot possibly win a conviction.

Should you go through with pressing charges? Do you have the emotional strength to tell about your attack in court? Will your family go along with your decision and support you? Will you feel safer with the rapist in jail? Do you want to help protect other victims from attack?

Many victims decide yes on all these counts. They are able to vent their anger by doing something about the attack rather than just trying to forget it. Many women see it as a way out of constant fear that the rapist will return. Others feel it is a courageous, moral act to help improve society for all women.

If both the DA and the victim decide to press charges:

STEP 5: PRELIMINARY HEARING

Usually within twenty-four to forty-eight hours after a suspect is arrested, he will face a preliminary hearing. One kind of hearing is held before a judge. The rapist and his attorney will be present; you will be asked to testify. The judge evaluates the evidence, and if he decides it's insufficient, he drops the case. If he decides the evidence warrants a full trial, the case will go to court.

Another type of preliminary hearing is a grand jury hearing. This hearing is held in court before a jury of people from the community. The rapist and his lawyer will not be present. You may or may not be asked to testify. Sometimes only the detective will present the facts of your case. This jury will then decide if there's enough evidence for a full trial.

After the hearing comes arraignment. During arraignment the judge informs the rapist of the charges against him and of his rights. The suspect then enters his guilty or not guilty plea. If he pleads guilty, the judge sets the date for sentencing. If he pleads not guilty, the judge orders a trial.

STEP 6: TRIAL

A trial date will be set and you will be notified. However, you can expect the actual trial to be postponed several times. Through such delays, the defense tries to wear you down. They hope you will change your mind about prosecuting or move away or be so nervous you will want to forget the entire thing.

The defense attorney may call you and ask you to drop the charges. If he does, you are not required to talk to him. (Ask the DA what to say if the defense lawyer tries to contact you.) Infrequently, the attacker himself or his family may try to contact you and try to talk you out of the charges. (The suspect will not have your address or phone number unless he had it prior to the attack.) You do not have to talk to either him or his family. If anyone makes threats, the judge will order them to stop and fine them if they don't. The police will offer protection.

Each time the date for your trial comes up, you will probably be anxious and worried. If you were not notified of the delay, you may waste time coming to the courthouse only to be told there will be a postponement and a new trial date. However, many DA's offices now try to give witnesses advance notice when there will be a delay.

During this time, plea bargaining may take place. In exchange for the rapist's pleading guilty to a lesser charge, the DA may bargain for a sure conviction to at least some charge. Depending on how strong he thinks the case will be, the DA will make the decision about letting the rapist plead guilty to a lesser charge.

Before the actual trial begins, the defendant chooses whether he would like to be tried before a judge or jury. Defendants almost always opt for a jury trial, because judges have heard all the defense tricks before and aren't impressed. Juries show more sympathy when defense attorneys tell how a conviction will ruin the "nice man's" reputation. Defendants also hope you will be embarrassed and more timid about giving details in front of a jury.

For years a rape trial was thought of as one of the most demoralizing, horrifying experiences a female could go through, often much worse than the rape itself. The work of women's groups across the country has greatly improved the situation. Going through any trial is a frightening, upsetting experience, but victims should be encouraged by the improvement in the trial process through new laws and policies.

At present, forty-two states have amended their rape laws to restrict questions about a victim's previous sexual history. In the past, the victim could be questioned about her past, but the previous arrests or convictions of the accused couldn't be mentioned in court. Now if for some reason such questioning of the victim is allowed, it is done in private chambers where the judge decides if it is relevant to the case.

A second change in the law dealing with rape is that a victim seidom has to prove she resisted to the utmost. In the past if the defendant claimed the woman agreed to have sex with him, the victim had to prove she fought him off. This was especially strange because police advised victims *not* to fight back and risk injury. Now, new laws put the burden of proof about whether a victim consented on the accused. He must prove that she did agree.

Many laws are changing rape charges to sexual assault charges and assessing penalties on degrees of assault and injury. In the past, most rape penalties were stiff—sometimes even death for a first offender. Juries were extremely reluctant to convict and give such a sentence. The result was that attackers escaped punishment. With lesser penalties and degrees for deciding penalties, juries are more willing to find the accused guilty.

When the actual trial date arrives, you will be called to appear in court. Many courts today have improved their handling of the victim's court appearance. Frequently, she is permitted to wait in a separate waiting room so she doesn't have to be around the defendant and his family. Instead of having to wait in court all day, the victim may be on call and notified just before her case comes up. Some courts make an effort to schedule all rape cases on the same day so that rape victims can give each other moral support.

When your case is called, you will take the stand. If others have been victims of the same rapist, all of you will testify. You will be asked to give your name, but you can omit your address.

During the trial questioning, the term "alleged" rape will be used. Don't let that upset or anger you. If the case is not called an "alleged" rape and the defendant is not referred to as the "accused" or a similar term rather than the attacker, the case can be dismissed because every defendant is innocent until proven guilty.

Your attorney will first question you about the attack and allow you to tell what happened. Then the defense attorney will question you. Your lawyer will have prepared you beforehand for the defense's tactics.

The defense attorney will base the defense on one of three points:

- identification—the defense will say the police caught the wrong man
- no actual rape—the defense will say that the defendant assaulted you but never completed the rape. (This defense is rarely used anymore. In states where the new laws have broadened "rape" to mean all kinds of sexual assault, the attacker will be subject to conviction, no matter how he assaulted you or how successful he was.)

- consent—the defense will say you consented to have sex with the defendant

If the defense attorney bases the case on mistaken identity, he or she will question you about how you could remember so well and how dark it was during the attack. He or she may point out that you were too upset to remember the defendant's face and how unobservant you are in other matters. (He may turn his back and ask if you remember what color tie he is wearing). He'll show how the defendant couldn't possibly have been at the crime scene at that particular time.

If the defense attorney bases his case on the claim that there was no actual rape, he will try to confuse you on the details of exactly what the accused said and did. He may make it appear that the man merely made a pass at you, and when you resisted, he left you alone.

If the defense bases the case on consent, the attorney will say that because you ride the same bus or live in the same apartment building, you and the man knew each other well and you agreed to have sex. The attorney may imply that your character is so bad that you would have sex with anyone, and you couldn't possibly accuse any man of rape. He may try to support this defense by attempting to prove that you are on drugs, that you constantly go to wild parties, and that you are truant from school. He may imply that you set up the accused, seduced him, and encouraged him to attack. Finally, he will try to paint the accused as an average American good guy, who couldn't possibly think of a crime like rape.

All of these defense questions and comments may be drenched with sarcasm, may be loud and angry, or may be made in a nice, cordial, condescending tone. Through all this, you must try to remain calm and answer the questions carefully, as you have been counseled by the DA. Remember that some defense cases are so weak that the defense attorney can't even put on a good show.

After you testify, others will take the stand. The police detective will present evidence from the investigation. Occasionally, the doctor who examined you will be called to testify. After the DA has presented your case, the defense may call character witnesses for the defendant to say what a nice guy he is. Only rarely will the accused take the stand. When he does, his defense attorney loses control of the questioning, and the DA can ask too many damaging questions.

Both lawyers will summarize their cases and then the jury (or judge) decides if the accused is guilty.

A verdict of not guilty doesn't mean that you weren't raped or that the jury thinks you were lying. It simply means that the jury didn't have enough evidence to convict "without reasonable doubt." Our legal system is devoted to the concept, "innocent until proven guilty." The burden of proof is always on the prosecutor and the victim. Some charges just cannot be proven without a reasonable doubt.

If the jury cannot reach a unanimous decision, it's called a hung jury and another trial date may be set, or the case may be dropped.

If the verdict is "guilty," the rapist will be sentenced at a later date. He is off the streets. You and others are free from any threats he may have made or any future attacks by him.

What have you gained from the legal process? Conviction rates are low. Statistics say that only 10 percent to 35 percent of all cases end in conviction of the accused. These statistics can be confusing. First, many convictions don't show up on the books as rape convictions because of plea bargaining. A rapist would rather plead guilty to burglary than to rape. The DA often accepts his offer to assure a conviction and to spare the victim the trial process. Some rape charges are dropped because the offender is guilty of a higher crime, such as murder. The DA tries him on murder charges to get a stiffer penalty. You should not be overly discouraged at rape conviction statistics, because they are not as low as some figures seem to indicate.

Others become discouraged when they hear of low penalties in rape cases. A convicted rapist serves an average of forty-four months, but light sentences are not the case in all states. Some states have the death penalty and others have maximums of thirty to fifty years imprisonment. Many law officers have suggested lighter sentences and mandatory psychiatric treatment as a way of getting more convictions.

While it is true that the legal process is at times slow and discouraging, it is the best mechanism we have to stop rape. Decide now that if you are ever a victim of rape, you will report the attack. If you have the courage, press charges and see your case through the courts. Your efforts will help eradicate rape and ensure safety for yourself and others.

CHAPTER *10*

Get Emotional Help

When you have a car accident, people hear about your injury and offer help in whatever way they can. With the physical and emotional injuries of rape, few people know about your problems and even fewer can help you adjust to the pain. If you have experienced rape and are fighting your way back to a normal life, perhaps reading this chapter about how other victims feel and cope can help you make your journey to adjustment.

Immediately after the rape, most victims experience constant fear—fear in realizing that they could have been brutalized or murdered and fear of the attacker's return. This fear prohibits many women from even reporting the attack to the police. If the attack was by an acquaintance, they fear upsetting some social relationship and the reaction of others among their family and friends.

A victim is often afraid even to go about her normal routine. She may be afraid to wait for the school bus at the corner. She may be afraid to return to her part-time job. She may be afraid to go outside to the mailbox. That the attacker may be watching and may attack again is always in the back of her mind.

If she has been attacked in an elevator, she may develop a phobia about riding elevators. She may develop a phobia about being home alone if the attack took place there. While walking down the street, she may constantly hear suspicious footsteps behind her. Her nights may be filled with nightmares about the attacker.

Some victims deal with this fear by trying to repress the fact that an attack really took place. Others deal with such fears by making all kinds of changes in their lives to protect themselves. They may transfer to another school or move to another town. They may change all the locks on their doors. The family may have its telephone number changed or unlisted. Such measures can offer some comfort to a victim who is desperately fighting to get in control of her life again, to feel safe and secure as she once did.

Another common reaction of rape victims is to feel guilty, to feel that somehow they were at fault for the attack. If raped by a stranger, the girl feels that she should have been more careful in some way. She should have walked down a busier street. She shouldn't have detoured through a certain part of town. She shouldn't have been so stupid as to believe the man's line. She shouldn't have stayed out later than her parents told her. She shouldn't have worn a certain dress. The girl feels this guilt even though its unwarranted. The Federal Commission on Crimes of Violence reports that in only 4 percent of rapes could any behavior by the victim be labeled as provoking or inviting the attack.

If someone else, such as a boyfriend, was hurt in the attack, the victim may feel even guiltier. Anne, whose boyfriend was killed when two attackers approached them as they started to get into their car in a parking lot, expressed her guilt feelings this way: "I felt I could have kept James from being killed. I feel like they only wanted to get me and had to get James out of the way."

When a victim is attacked by an acquaintance, the guilt sometimes grows worse. With a stranger attack, the girl can see herself as merely an object and the attack as impersonal. But if the rapist is someone she knows, she questions herself about what she might have done to have encouraged the attack. Some victims who, out of fear, didn't resist feel guilty that they didn't fight harder and receive more injury.

Along with this sense of guilt, the victim often feels dirty, embarrassed, or immoral. This feeling probably comes from the often accepted idea that "good" girls don't get raped. The victim keeps lamenting the attack as if it were a blot on her character. She feels that everybody must know about the rape and be staring at her as if she were a freak.

These feelings of fear, guilt, and embarrassment can even show themselves in physical ways: nausea, cramps, muscle soreness, insomnia.

A victim's primary defense to free herself of this guilt and fear is to try to forget the attack. She tries to resume her normal routine and reassure her family and friends that she has adjusted.

Dealing with the reactions of parents and friends, however, sometimes complicates this effort to forget and adjust. Some parents keep talking about the incident over and over, hoping that talking through the emotional hurt will get the daughter's fears out in the open. Some parents, especially fathers, become enraged at the attacker and want him punished immediately. Some parents blame their daughter, saying she should have been more careful.

Parents usually do this out of a sense of their own guilt. They feel that they should have been able to protect you from the attack, that they have failed in their parental responsibilities. If they know the attacker, they feel even more responsible for not recognizing warning signs.

When parents feel guilty, they overreact by trying to monitor your every activity. The teen years are a time when young people need to develop their own independence. They are trying to pull away from their parents and see if they can make it on their own. Rape changes that struggle. Teens feel ambivalent about wanting their parents' protection, and at the same time wanting to prove that they can take care of themselves, even in a world that includes rape. Such a struggle between a teen and her parents can develop into serious communication problems.

Both the victim and her parents try to blame someone or something for the attack, Dr. Martin Symonds, psychiatrist, professor of psychiatry at New York University School of Medicine, says, because they feel safer. If they can figure out a real or imagined cause for the rape, they can remove the cause and reassure themselves that such an attack will never be repeated. When rape appears to happen randomly, they feel helpless about the future.

While you may primarily be reacting to the horror and violence of the rape, fathers and boyfriends often focus on the rape as a sexual act. They feel rage and insult, as if they had been personally attacked. Friends may question you about the attack. The experience is frightening to them and has much the same attraction as a ghost story. Sometimes friends show no reaction at all; they have no idea what you are going through.

Fear, guilt, embarrassment, depression, parents and friends' reactions—how do you deal with all of it?

Sometimes you can work through these feelings on your own. With a great deal of effort, you can sometimes put fear out of your mind. By reading articles and books like this one, you can reassure yourself that you were in no way to blame for the attack and that you should have no guilt feelings or embarrassment. You may want to enroll in self-defense classes to reassure yourself about your safety in the future. Time will usually help with handling family and friends' reactions. Your task will be an uphill battle. Working through a rape experience goes faster and easier when you have outside help.

That's where rape crisis centers come into the picture. Thanks to volunteer staffs, many cities across the country now have these centers. (You can find them in the Yellow Pages under "Women's Services" or "Women's Organizations." If you have trouble finding the listing, call the library and ask for the rape crisis center hotline number.)

Girls who know about the rape crisis centers may call immediately after an assault. Workers there can advise where to get the best medical treatment for rape, tell you about social services that might help pay for treatment, and refer you to counseling services within or outside their center. If your city doesn't have a center, you can phone the National Organization for the Prevention of Rape and Assault (NOPRA, (212) 371-3664) and they will refer you to a local counselor, doctor, or lawyer.

If you have been attacked and have no one to go to the hospital with you for the medical exam, a rape crisis center volunteer will accompany you and help you through the process. She will also go through the police reporting procedures with you. A parent will have to sign for medical treatment, but your parent, too, might welcome help with the exam and the reporting.

Rape crisis centers provide much more than referral services. Volunteers can help in both your emotional and physical adjustment. Their help is especially beneficial if you cannot talk to your parents about the rape. Teen volunteers who themselves have been rape victims can also share their readjustment experiences with you and help you work through some of the same problems with friends, family, and school.

The counseling done through rape centers is primarily done by the telephone. This saves you time, and it assures you of privacy and freedom to control the counseling. You do not need to identify yourself if you feel embarrassed. If at any time you want to end the conversation, you are free to hang up. Counselors will never call your home without your permission and will never identify themselves in a way that might embarrass you. There is never any pressure to tell anything about the rape that you don't want to mention. There's never pressure to file charges against your attacker.

What the rape crisis center does offer is someone who cares about and understands what you are going through. They can help you reorganize your life and pull yourself together enough to go back to school or to work. They know that the sooner you are able to get back to your normal routine, the sooner you can reach emotional readjustment.

The volunteers at the center can help you handle any adverse reactions from your family or friends. The staff members even encourage family members to call and get advice on how they can best help you. If you have decided to press charges against the rapist, they can help explain the police investigation and trial process. They can help you sort out your feelings about men, dating, and sex. If you're interested, they can tell you about good self-defense courses.

Of course, all these things can't be discussed on your first phone call. You may need to call them several times over a period of weeks or months after the attack. If you prefer office visits, they can arrange those for you.

How much counseling you need depends on your own emotional strength, how supportive your family and friends are, and what physical and legal processes you are going through. The earlier you take advantage of their counseling, the sooner you can begin to get your life back in order.

This aid will carry you to the last leg of your journey— the period of final adjustment. After having replayed the attack over and over in your mind, you finally are able to rid yourself of any guilt. By forcing yourself to get out and go places and do things, you rationally work through your paralyzing fears and decide how to live in a world that contains violence. You try to categorize men individually rather than as a group and learn to relate to them again.

Despite the difficulty of the journey to adjustment, you are not damaged for life. Victims across the country testify that you *can* survive emotionally. Call a rape crisis center for help along the way. Perhaps by becoming a volunteer yourself in a rape crisis center or involving yourself in a constructive anti-rape program, you can help resolve some of your fears and guilts.

PART FOUR

What About the Future?

CHAPTER *11*

When the Molester is Someone in Your Family

Incest is the term for sexual intercourse between relatives; "relatives" are usually defined by law to mean a relationship closer than first cousins. Because incest is a taboo subject in all cultures, you seldom hear the term or the act discussed. That doesn't mean that incestuous relationships don't go on in all cultures. In ancient Egypt, brother and sister incest was permitted in order to breed a pure-blooded ruling family. Cleopatra married her brother. Nowadays, incest is occasionally mentioned in TV shows, movies, and magazines. Despite certain ancient and modern exceptions to the taboo, incest has always been a dangerous, unhealthy activity.

If you are caught in a sexually abusive situation at home, this chapter should help you understand what has led to the relationship, what harm may come from it, how it can be stopped, and how your family situation can be improved.

The majority of Americans are just now becoming aware of how widespread incest is. In a recent survey taken of its readership, *Cosmopolitan* magazine found that 10 percent of all women responding to their survey on sex said they had had incestuous relationships.

Counselors like David Walters and Rita and Blair Justice, who have worked extensively with families involved in incest, support these figures and conclude that as few as one in twenty cases is ever reported. If you are part of an incestuous relationship, you are not alone.

If incest is a taboo and psychologically unhealthy, why is it so common? Psychologists tell us that incest is an excess or misdirection of a basic need in all persons—to feel closeness, warmth, love, and belonging in a family.

Modern society and family life-styles often contribute to incest. Sex is seen together by the family on television, and often is the subject of jokes. Pornographic magazines, television, and movies sometimes highlight incest. Modern permissive attitudes toward sex probably have an effect on incestuous relationships, but they do not explain incest, which has been around since ancient civilizations. Primarily individual family relationships and circumstances contribute to the problem. For instance, in many poorer families, family members are thrown together in crowded quarters, and brothers and sisters must often share a bed.

Brothers often assault their sisters in a home where parents are weak disciplinarians, are preoccupied, or spend too much time away from home. Sometimes the brother who has no outside friends is so lonely that he turns to his sister for sexual love. Then these brothers threaten their sisters with violence if they tell. Often, a brother will start such a relationship before the younger sister knows what is going on and that the situation is unnatural and unhealthy. When the girl does realize that this is not a normal relationship, she already feels guilty about her role in the situation. Brothers play on that guilt to keep the girl quiet. In the vast majority of cases, however, when the girl understands what's happening and tells her parents, they can put a stop to it without outside help.

When a father or stepfather is doing the assaulting, the situation is harder for most girls to deal with. Special family circumstances foster the problem. The father and mother usually have a poor or nonexistent sex life. Perhaps the mother is sick or away from home much of the time or keeps different hours from her husband. The father finds himself at home alone with his daughter too much of the time.

A stepfather may join a family when the daughter is beginning to be a physically attractive woman. He may not be used to the father role, and the only way he knows how to handle females is in a sexually seductive way. He disciplines her or gets her to cooperate with family rules by flirting with her. When they are thrown together under the same roof all the time, he may develop a sexual attraction for her.

Whatever the situation in your home—whether a brother, father, or stepfather is assaulting you—the relationship is a very damaging one for both you and the other person. The longer the relationship lasts, the greater the damage. In the past, the harm was thought mainly to be physical—birth defects, mental retardation, and so forth. Today psychologists have uncovered much more evidence about psychological and emotional harm to the entire family, as well as to the victim. A study done by the American Humane Association showed that two-thirds of the victims were emotionally damaged, 14 percent severely disturbed.

How old a victim is has a lot to do with the amount of damage she suffers. A young child doesn't realize the significance of sex and doesn't feel much guilt or attach much importance to the situation. An older girl is much more aware of the sexual significance. She learns that all fathers and daughters don't behave in this manner. She feels depression and guilt and has a very low self-image. Sometimes these feelings lead a girl to drugs, prostitution, or even suicide. A young child feels love and even sexual attraction for her father. By the age of six or seven, a girl normally moves beyond these feelings and continues to develop a nonsexual, loving relationship with her father. When she gets sex instead, she feels used and confused. Often a father refuses to let the girl have friends her own age, and her normal personality development becomes stunted.

A future marriage can be affected by a young girl's previous incestuous experiences. She feels she can't trust her husband. She thinks that he is unreliable and immature. Their sex life is often not satisfying because of her past involvement and guilt feelings about sex. Mothers in a home where there is incest are usually passive. They suffer threats and a poor marital relationship in silence. The daughter's marriage will also be affected if she models herself after a passive mother.

Not only daughters suffer from such a relationship—the entire family does. Family members do not relate to each other as a normal family. The daughter usually gets special favors and privileges from her father, which causes the other children to feel jealous. The whole family remains isolated from outside friends who are necessary to normal mental health. Both parents suffer in that they fail to deal with and resolve their marriage problems.

If you are involved in this kind of relationship, be assured that you are not to blame, no matter how willingly you originally participated in the sexual relationship. Keep in mind that you were acting normally; your father was not. Parents are supposed to be mature, and they should know that such a relationship is damaging to you. Part of their responsibility is to see that no such situation develops, that sex plays no part in a loving father-daughter relationship. If you flirt with your father, as most girls do, he is not supposed to flirt back. Fathers aren't supposed to let you sleep in the same bed with them; they shouldn't walk around naked in front of you or touch you in sexual ways.

Parents are supposed to let you be a child. They are supposed to set the limits for your behavior and help you build self-esteem. They should give you affection in non-sexual ways, encourage you to separate from them and have friends your own age, and, in general, be good role models for you.

Most girls become aware of the damaging results of incest by the time they reach their teen years. The problem is that they don't know what to do. They feel trapped and guilty about being involved in such a relationship. If they tell their mother or an outsider, they fear they will be blamed for the relationship. Sometimes they fear their father's reaction if they tell.

Many girls remain silent for reasons other than guilt. Some continue the relationship with their father to try to keep the family together. Sometimes the family is full of hostility. The mother and father don't get along and don't have a good sexual relationship with each other. The father seems restless, unhappy, and ready to leave home. Despite all the father may have done, the daughter may still feel love for and loyalty to him. She fears that outsiders will turn on him and that he may be put in jail. She thinks her mother will be heartbroken and that the marriage will end. The daughter feels compelled to try in any way she can to keep the family together.

Other girls remain silent and keep up the relationship to protect younger sisters. Many girls who reach their teens see the harm in the situation and feel very bitter toward their fathers. But they continue to keep quiet about it, thinking that if the father keeps assaulting them, he will leave their sisters alone. Research shows, however, that fathers who molest one daughter will eventually or simultaneously molest all. Sisters often do not dare bring the subject up with each other until much later in life. When they do, they usually find out that their father had molested them all and has only led them to believe he was leaving the others alone.

If you have permitted sexual assault from your father for any reason, it is understandable and common. But no reason is good enough to let the relationship continue. Forcing the situation out in the open is the best thing you can do for everyone concerned.

When you do tell someone and ask for help, you'll undoubtedly face some immediate problems. There will probably be anger from your father, and even from your mother. You will have to be convinced from the very beginning that you are doing the right thing for all of you.

Understanding the how and why behind your parents' reactions will help you cope with the ordeal. Your father probably functions fairly well in society. The majority of fathers who assault their daughters hold good jobs and are usually well-respected in society. However, in close personal relationships, they do not function normally.

A father's assault shows deep hostility toward his wife. This poor relationship often stems from childhood problems he has brought with him into his marriage. Your father may have been alone a lot as a child. Perhaps his father was seldom home or didn't show him much affection. His mother, too, may have rejected him and showed little affection. In other words, your father is still acting like a child trying to get someone to love him—you—and make up for what he missed in a normal childhood.

Other fathers may assault their daughters out of anger for how they have been treated by women. They want to get even with women in general. They do this by being unfaithful to a wife or by using and harming a daughter.

Most of the time, a father feels extremely guilty for what he is doing to his daughter. A few fathers rationalize their behavior to avoid feeling so guilty. Counselors Rita and Blair Justice, through their counseling with fathers, have discovered quite a list of "reasons" fathers give for molesting daughters.

Some men convince themselves that their children are their property and have no rights of their own. They think that what they do with their property is nobody's business. Some fathers rationalize that teaching their daughters about sex in this way is their parental duty and responsibility. Some even think they are protecting a daughter from taking up with the wrong kind of boys. Other fathers claim that they are sexually free and that they don't want their daughters inhibited about sex. Fathers who don't have any rationalization for the relationship blame alcohol or memory loss for the assaults.

No matter what the motivation behind your father's assaults, he can only be helped by counseling. Your father may very well react violently, make you feel like a traitor, or act guilty and hurt; but you must remember that telling someone else is for the good of both of you.

You probably are not sure whom to tell.

First consider telling your mother. Find a time when your talk will not be interrupted. You might start the conversation something like this: "Mother, I want to talk to you about something that's been upsetting me a lot. It's about something that Daddy has been doing (or did) to me and I wish you could stop it. Sometimes late at night (or, sometimes when you're gone), he . . . " Once you get into the subject, your mother will probably help you get the details out by asking you questions. If she has no idea that your father has been assaulting you, she will be shocked and disappointed in him. If she confronts the situation honestly, she will face many difficulties. People may blame her for forcing the situation into the open. They may not remain friendly with her any longer. If the marriage breaks up, she may have to take over the financial responsibility for the family. Through this difficult time, you and your mother may develop a new closeness.

But your mother may not *want* to hear the truth. Many girls have hinted to their mothers about the sexual assaults and have found that their mothers wanted to disbelieve or ignore the problem. A mother may actually be glad about the situation because she no longer has to have sexual relations with her husband. On the other hand, she may want to help you, but she may feel weak and unable to stop the situation. She may feel that she needs your father for financial security and she can't offend him. She may even stay away from home more often so she doesn't have to face the facts. If your mother behaves like this, then you will need to ask an outsider for help.

A mother or father who refuses to get help is like the young child who wants to avoid taking medicine for an infection. Even though he feels sick, he thinks the medicine is worse than the illness. In his immaturity, he can't see that a few seconds of unpleasantness are worth eventual good health. Sometimes parents act like that about ailing family relationships. You may have to be the mature one and seek help from someone outside your family.

Any one of several outsiders can help you. You may feel close to another relative whom you can tell—an aunt or a grandparent. You might want to see a school counselor or a clergyman. The important thing is that you choose someone you can trust and someone who has the ability to help you.

Girls sometimes find that these outsiders already have some ideas about what's going on at home. The Justices point out that families in trouble give out clues. Family members have their roles reversed in front of others. The father and mother act like the children, while the daughter has to take the parents' responsibility. Sometimes outsiders pick up clues when the mother shows jealousy. Others may have noticed that your father restricts your friendships and is overly cautious about whom you go out with. Brothers and sisters may show jealousy about the special treatment you receive. You, as a daughter, probably give off clues about your unhappiness, such as depression, a poor self-image, uninvolvement with kids of your own age, or secretiveness about family life.

If you decide not to tell a family member or a family friend, a minister or a school counselor, you may call the child welfare department whose number is listed in the phone book. Ask to talk to a social worker about their child-protective services.

Things may be rough at home for a while. Being sure that you are doing the best thing for your own mental and physical health will give you the courage to get help.

If your mother stands by you, she may ask your father to leave home, or dissolve their marriage, or file charges against him. Instead of legal action, she may seek counseling for all of you by contacting the welfare department or a private counselor. You two will have to discuss your feelings and see what seems best in your family situation.

If your mother refuses to stop the situation, you or whoever you ask for help will have to report the assaults to the child welfare department. The social worker will investigate the situation and determine what seems best. The social worker's primary aim is to keep families together, not to punish your father. He or she will arrange for your whole family, including your father, to begin counseling sessions to teach you a new way of relating to each other.

If your father or mother refuses to enter counseling, the social worker has the authority to remove you from the home. Sometimes families change their living arrangements themselves. You can make arrangements to live somewhere else or your father may want to leave. If you cannot make other living arrangements, the social worker will help by placing you in a foster home or other temporary living quarters.

Legal charges against your father are a last resort. Although fathers are often reluctant to go for help, when faced with possible legal action, they choose counseling. If your mother decides to file charges, there may or may not be a trial. Some law officers and attorneys estimate that about 80 to 90 percent of fathers plead guilty to the charges without a trial. Depending on the extent of his assaults and his intentions to correct the situation, your father will probably be given probation with the alternative of attending therapy sessions.

This therapy can help all family members see the harm in the incestuous relationship. A counselor will help your parents improve their marital relationship and show them how to handle stress situations such as those arising from financial worries and sickness, which often contribute to the problem. The counselor will encourage all family members to build friendships outside the family and to become involved in outside activities.

If your father is an alcoholic, the counselor will encourage him to get help through Alcoholics Anonymous.

For support in making a change in your family, encourage your parents to join Parents United, an organization of parents trying to overcome this problem. For your own emotional support, contact Daughters and Sons United, the teen organization of this parental group.

Therapy will change and improve life for you and your entire family.

Sexual assault in your home can be the most damaging kind. It can destroy your present and future happiness by making you feel guilty, depressed, insecure, and unworthy of love. It can prevent you from building necessary friendships among your peers and can destroy your chances for happy dating and marriage.

Tell someone you trust about the situation and get help for your family. Your health and happiness depend on it.

CHAPTER 12

Why You Shouldn't Forget

A mirror broken off your car. The garage door pried open and your tennis racket stolen. Lunch money lifted from your locker during gym. These incidents can be explained as random attacks by dishonest people. They can be forgotten.

Your name scribbled with obscenities on the bathroom wall at school. A whispered threat on the telephone. A slap in the face by an angry boyfriend. These things are harder to forget: they are personal attacks.

Rape is different still. Some have called it an invasion of the ego. A violent attack on your psyche, your emotions, and your body, rape can hang over your head for the rest of your life. As you move back into your normal activities and begin to relate again to people outside your family, the load becomes lighter. Nevertheless, the experience never completely disappears from your subconscious mind.

Trying to forget the rape provides a good release from tension and fear. Forgetting enables you to resume your normal life. But after time has helped you to readjust to school and social routines, then you can more comfortably remember the incident.

Remembering is what this chapter is all about.

Not forgetting the rape experience can help you and other victims change society. To change society does seem an overwhelming task. Yet, like each impossible project that's ever been completed, change begins with small segments. You begin to change society when you change the people you know—the people you go to school with and work with, your family, and your neighbors.

First, you work to change people's ideas about rape. Rape is violence, not sexual passion. Many rapists have a deep-seated hate of women, while others merely see an opportunity to exploit someone without being caught. Rape degrades, horrifies, and brutalizes.

Rapists are of all races and all social and economic classes. No one is immune from rape assaults—not the very young, not the very old. Girls can't stay home to avoid rape; they lead an active life. Even girls who do stay home are not safe, because almost half of the attacks occur in the home. Rape can happen to any female, and it happens often.

Doesn't society realize all this? No, it doesn't. In movies, novels, television and conversation, rape is treated all too often as a joke. Rape attacks have become so frequent that society is desensitized. Many people have developed a "so-what?" attitude. One teenager expressed her exasperation at this attitude:

> This custodian has attacked several girls here (an after-school gymnastics class in a local health club). When their mothers drop them off early and they walk over to the coke machines across the street, he catches them

outside. Or, when some of the classes aren't over until eight and they walk home alone. When I first started lessons, several of the girls warned me to stay away from him. But nobody tells their mother because they don't want to have to stop coming to classes. They figure that they can keep away from him. But we have told the manager of the gym. You know what he said? How concerned he is? "Yeah, we've had some complaints. But we can't find anybody else to work these hours and clean up the place. Maybe we can let him go when summer comes and we can get some college kid to take his place." Now that's real concern. Can you imagine that?

People like the manager are not the only ones to blame for an attitude that promotes sexual assault. Those who deal in pornography play a large part. As mentioned in Chapter 5, pornographic magazines and movies tell men that women are property to be exploited. As many convicted rapists have admitted, such material even gives them ideas for trapping and brutalizing victims.

To change people's attitudes about rape, you have to talk and work. Talk to your girlfriends about safety. Use your influence in clubs and school organizations to establish and promote safety precautions. Ask school leaders and counselors for better lighting in walkways and study areas, more security guards, and emergency telephones installed in strategic places away from the main school building.

Print and distribute brochures and fliers on safety techniques, rape reporting procedures, and rape crisis center services. Ask businesspeople in your city to furnish the paper and copying equipment for the fliers. Many businesses, such as real estate offices and savings and loan companies, help with such services as good public relations. If such brochures are already available through the police, use your club members to distribute them.

Help start classes in self-defense. Contact your school counselor about setting them up during school hours. If he or she can't help, talk to an officer in the parent-teacher organization in your school district. Any time you can get an adult to help you with such plans, leadership people in the community will react more favorably. If something can't be worked out in your school system, contact the physical education department at a nearby college, the YMCA, or the police department. All of these groups offer such classes from time to time.

Encourage kids you run around with to report acts of violence and suspicious incidents or people. Never assume that someone else has already reported two strange-looking "repairmen" on campus. Work with your school counselor or student council to set up peer policing systems to eliminate campus attacks. Make it easy for students to report, anonymously if necessary, campus violence to school authorities.

Along with peer policing programs, several schools have organized peer counseling programs. Volunteer student counselors are trained for a period of a few weeks and then voluntarily maintain offices or hotlines at school to counsel students who are reluctant to talk to adults. Such a counseling service helps in two ways: it can direct a rape victim to other services where she can get help, and it may help potential rapists deal with their emotional problems before it's too late.

Establish or work with already existing women's consciousness-raising groups. Such organizations deal with the stresses females face in school and at work. These groups often take the lead in political action. If you don't have such an organization in your area, work through existing clubs. Volunteer to provide programs and get speakers when needed. You can contact professionals from the business community like gynecologists, lawyers, psychiatrists, police officers, or rape crisis center workers to give talks on rape and rape prevention and mental health services offered in your area.

When plans to build a special youth center are discussed among leaders in your community, make your voice heard. Promote such efforts so that boys have a constructive place to go and aren't tempted to form violent gangs out of sheer boredom.

Encourage and help women leaders in your area to form rape crisis centers. Such groups often begin as an extension of an already organized agency like a hospital, mental health center, or YWCA. Contact women in these groups and ask for names of people who might take on the project. Patrick Mills' book, *Rape Intervention Resource Manual* (Charles C. Thomas Publishing Co., Springfield, Illinois, 1977) provides a detailed guide to getting such a center started.

Get addresses of other crisis centers across the nation from the library and write for their brochures on how to establish a rape crisis center. After gathering all the materials, present your results to an adult who will adopt your project. Volunteer to help organize the program and answer the telephones when counseling services are started. If your city already has such a center, volunteer to answer their crisis calls.

Don't forget political action. Write letters to members of congress about changing and improving laws. Letters bring results, and the more letters you can encourage others to write, the better.

Review Chapter 9 about the legal aspects of rape. Know about the new laws passed in some states regarding degrees of sexual assault, the proper questioning of victims, and the sentence length and mandatory psychiatric treatment for the rapist. Call or visit the library to find out what the laws in your state say. Then let your congressman or congresswoman know about changes that need to be made.

Don't forget about laws governing pornography. Write to Citizens for Decency Through Law, 450 Leader Building, Cleveland, Ohio 44114, for details about how to help change laws regarding pornographic materials. This organization, founded by dissenting members of the President's Commission on Obscenity and Pornography, is anxious to make known the effects of pornography in society.

Locally, you can voice objections about pornography by writing to the editor of the newspaper and complaining about x-rated movies shown in your community. Junior high students in Oxnard, California, recently picketed a theater in a local shopping center because of its x-rated movies. The owner of the shopping center filed suit to have the x-rated movies stopped. Many newspapers will not accept ads for such movies. If your letters are effective, a lack of advertising for such movies will minimize the influence they can have on people in your area.

Remember that despite all the energy and good ideas young people have to offer, the world still revolves around adult leadership. Contact all the adults you can to help with your plans involving the entire community. However, the school campus is your domain. It provides a big arena where you can work effectively with minimal adult guidance.

Don't forget that society changes one step at a time. Start with your friends.

Remember rape so that others won't have to.

Bibliography

Amir, Menachim. *Patterns in Forcible Rape.* Chicago: University of Chicago Press, 1971.

Angel, S. "Don't Be Afraid to Say No!" *Redbook,* July, 1978, p. 40.

"Arguing about Death for Rape." *Time,* April 11, 1977, p. 80.

Bennett, Vivo, and Clagett, Cricket. *1001 Ways to Avoid Getting Mugged, Murdered, Robbed, Raped or Ripped Off.* New York: Mason/Charter, 1977.

Bode, Janet. *Fighting Back: How to Cope with the Medical, Emotional and Legal Consequences of Rape.* New York: Macmillan, 1978.

Bode, Janet. *Rape: Preventing It, Coping with the Legal, Medical, and Emotional Aftermath.* New York: Franklin Watts Publishers, 1979.

Brownmiller, Susan. *Against Our Will: Men, Women and Rape.* New York: Simon and Schuster, 1975.

Burgess, Ann W., and Holmstrom, Lynda L. *Rape: Victims of Crisis.* Bowie, Massachusetts: Brady, 1974.

Bush, S. "Putting the Victim's Sex Life on Trial," *Psychology Today,* December 1977, p. 152.

Chappell, Duncan; Geis, Robley; and Geis, Gilbert, eds. *Forcible Rape: The Crime, the Victim, and the Offender.* New York: Columbia University Press, 1977.

"Child's Garden of Perversity." *Time,* April 4, 1977. pp. 55–56.

Cohen, D. R. "To Avoid Rape, Be Ready To Struggle at Home." *Psychology Today,* November 1978, pp. 124–125.

Cottle, Thomas J. *Children's Secrets.* Garden City, New York: Doubleday, 1980.

Cross, Susan C. *The Rights of Women: An American Civil Liberties Union Handbook.* New York: Sunrise Books, 1973.

Cryer, Dr. Linda; and Cryer, P. H.; and McDowell, Jennifer H. "Rape Prevention." *Your Health,* February 1980, pp. 4–8.

De Francis, Vincent. *Protecting the Child Victim of Sex Crimes Committed by Adults.* Denver: American Humane Association, 1969.

Drakeford, Dr. John W., and Hamm, Jack. *Pornography: The Sexual Mirage.* Nashville: Thomas Nelson, 1973.

Gager, Nancy, and Shurr, Cathleen. *Sexual Assault: Confronting Rape in America.* New York: Grosset and Dunlap, 1976.

"Guilty Victims, Theories of M. Symonds." *Newsweek,* June 17, 1974. p. 66.

Halpern, Susan. *Rape: Helping the Victim.* Oradell, N.J.: Medical Economics Company, 1978.

Hilberman, Elaine, M.D. *The Rape Victim.* New York: Basic Books, 1976.

Horos, Carol V. *Rape.* New Canaan, Connecticut: Tobey Publishing, 1974.

Hursch, Carolyn J. *The Trouble With Rape.* Chicago: Nelson, 1977.

Hyde, Margaret O. *Speak Out on Rape.* New York: McGraw-Hill, 1976.

Justice, Rita, and Justice, Blair. *The Broken Taboo: Sex in the Family.* New York: Human Sciences Press, 1979.

Keerdoja, E., and Simons, P. E. "Strong Convictions: Views of Former Judge A. Simonson." *Newsweek,* September 11, 1968, p. 14.

MacKellar, Jean. *Bait and the Trap.* New York: Crown, 1975.

Medea, Andra, and Thompson, Kathleen. *Against Rape.* New York: Farrar, Straus and Giroux, 1974.

Mills, Patrick, ed. *Rape Intervention Resource Manual.* Springfield, Illinois: Charles C. Thomas, 1977.

Moira, A., and Rule, A. "It Happened to Me." *Good Housekeeping,* May 1978, p. 10.

National Institute of Law Enforcement and Criminal Justice Law Enforcement Assistance Administration, U.S. Department of Justice. *Forcible Rape: Medical and Legal Information.* Washington,

D.C.: U.S. Government Printing Office, Grant No. 76 NI 990056, October 1977.

Neier, A. "Rape at Home." *Nation,* January 20, 1979, pp. 36–37.

"Rape and Death: Supreme Court Decision on Death Penalty in Rape Cases," *Newsweek,* July 11, 1977, p. 48.

Rape and Its Victims: A Report for Citizens, Health Facilities, and Criminal Justice Agencies. Washington: Law Enforcement Assistance Administration of U.S. Department of Justice, 1975.

"Rape: The Crime Against Women." *Ladies Home Journal,* March 1977, p. 69.

Roucek, Joseph S. *Topics of Our Times No. 13: Sexual Attack, and the Crime of Rape.* Charlotteville, New York: Sam Har Press, 1975.

Sanford, Linda Tschirhart, and Fetter, Ann. *In Defense of Ourselves.* Garden City, New York: Doubleday, 1979.

Schwartz, M. D., and Clear, T. R. "Rape Law Reform and Women's Equality." *USA Today,* November 1979, pp. 35–37.

Simonson, A. "Rape and Culture: Controversial Views of A. Simonson." *Time,* September 12, 1977. p. 41.

Storaska, Frederick. *How to Say No to a Rapist—and Survive.* New York: Random House, 1975.

Swindler, A. "Some Thoughts on Rape." *Commonweal,* February 3, 1978, pp. 75–78.

Texas Department of Public Safety. *Crime in Texas.* Austin, Texas, 1978.

Walters, David R. *Physical and Sexual Abuse of Children: Causes and Treatment.* Bloomington: Indiana University Press, 1975.

Yates, Martha. *Coping: A Survival Manual for Women Alone.* Englewood Cliffs, New Jersey: Prentice-Hall, 1976.

Pamphlets

Assault on Women: Rape and Wife Beating. Public Affairs Pamphlet No. 579. January 1980.

Rape: Ideas for Self-Protection. Texas Crime Prevention Institute.

Rape: Lady Beware. Los Angeles, California Police Department.

Rape Prevention. City of Houston Health Department.

Target for Rape. Houston Police Department.

Index

364.1
BOO X

About the Author

Dianna Booher holds a BA degree from North Texas State University and a MA degree from the University of Houston, both degrees in English literature. She has worked extensively with young people, both as a teacher in public schools and together with her husband, who is a church youth director.

Ms. Booher has published religious curriculum materials as well as numerous magazine articles and short stories. She has published three teen self-help books, *Coping . . . When Your Family Falls Apart, Help, We're Moving* and *The Faces of Death,* and a novel *Not Yet Free.* A second novel, *Statistics,* will be out soon. Ms. Booher also conducts business writing workshops with her own firm, Booher Writing Consultants. Reviewing books for the Houston Chronicle rounds out her writing activities.

Dianna lives in Houston, Texas, with her husband, Dan, and two children, Jeffrey and Lisa.